FIVE FINGERS REVIEW 19

Skin

Five Fingers Review 19

BERKELEY ○ 2001

GENERAL EDITOR: Jaime Robles

EDITORS: Eileen O Malley Callahan, Renata Ewing, Denise Newman, and Linda Norton

PROOFREADING: Lisa Rappoport

TYPESETTING: Woodland Graphics, San Leandro

PRINTING: McNaughton-Gunn

Five Fingers Review is an annual publication of Five Fingers Press, a not-for-profit foundation. This issue is made possible through funding from the California Arts Council and the Zellerbach Family Fund. We would also like to thank our subscribers for their support.

Five Fingers Review is distributed by Small Press Distribution. Subscription queries should be addressed to *Five Fingers Review,* 652 Woodland Avenue, San Leandro, CA 94577.

All editorial correspondence should be addressed to:
Five Fingers Review
P.O. Box 12955
Berkeley, CA 94712-3955
e-mail: jrobles@best.com

ISBN: 1-880627-08-6

Printed and bound in the USA.

Cover art: Gigi Janchang
Cover design: Jaime Robles

Contents

•

"Almost Nothing Yet the Fragile
Amplitude of the World," selected by EILEEN O MALLEY CALLAHAN

•

•

A note from the editor

In 1869 a painting by Gabriel von Max entitled Der Anatom *(The Anatomist) was shown at the international art exhibition in Munich. In it, a young woman lies dead, waiting to be dissected by an anatomist. The woman's supine body lies horizontally across the bottom half of the canvas. She is young, and quite beautiful, her auburn hair lying in waves around her pale face. That face is inclined slightly toward the viewer: her eyes are closed, and her lips retain a rosy blush, as if she may have at that very second passed from life to death. A very white cloth is draped over her body and wraps around her feet, giving them a mummy-like quality. To the right of her covered knees a moth has lit on the dark table where she lies. Behind her sits a man, dressed in what we would consider formal dress, a dark suit. Around him and the draped figure is darkness. He appears barely emerged from shadow. He is looking at the woman in a contemplative manner, his hand to his chin. To his right and above the head of the dead woman we perceive the surfaces of a desk, books, the gleam of white pages, the clutter of scholarly research, the dull round sur-faces of eyeless skull. All of this canvas would exist as a kind of* memento mori, *a reminder of the ubiquitousness and inevitability of death, except for two details: the flush of red on the corpse's mouth and the man's right hand which is lifting the sheet away from the woman's body, exposing her breast. This hand is placed by the painter almost centrally in the canvas.**

It is this hand that reminds us that her body will be touched. That this man, who in life would be crossing some moral and ethical boundary by running his hand across a strange woman's bare skin, will not only be touching that skin but breaching its intactness. In fact, his main purpose is to breach that skin, to cut through its separating surface in order to examine and record what lies beneath and within it. The moth that lies near the woman's body is emblematic of the painter's belief that what lies beneath the surface of skin is more than physical matter, that beneath that surface swims a soul.

---

*For a more detailed analysis of this painting, see *Over Her Dead Body: Death, femininity and the aesthetic* by Elisabeth Bronfen, New York: Routledge, 1992, pp. 1–12.

Looking at anatomical drawings of about the same time, we see organs, networks of arteries and veins, all elaborately examined and recorded. The bodies that hold these organs are also meticulously drawn, but there is something artificial about the areas of the body that are depicted with the skin intact. It is as if the figures are no longer human, unlike the organs they contain, but rather marble statues or neoclassical paintings— skin and form have been idealized and thereby made less human.

Today, seeing beneath the skin is an everyday occurence. Anatomical drawings, surgical movies are easily obtainable. The discovery of uranium in 1899 made it possible to look beneath the surface of the skin. Pictured in ghostly whites on dark films, organs and bones can be examined, and the mysteries of our physicality read and interpreted. Without knives and without the presence of death. Skin itself, however, maintains an element of mystery—a mystery born of desire and the need to insert our consciousness into the life of the desired, to get under their skin, psychically and thereby physically.

A biologist perhaps would describe the millions of nerve cells that compose our skin, and explain how touch and eroticism are part of our reproductive need. Part of the urge of the species to continue life, to conquer death through the shuffling, reshuffling, and passing on of our genetic data. But how did that evolutionary fact become so elaborated with so many forms of desire? Through desire are we simply reenacting the dance that two cells make when they merge? When one cell breaks through the membrane that individualizes the other and its own skin dissolves?

Skin divides us from each other and from the surrounding world. It's hydrophobic, like the Wicked Witch of the West. Without that quality of repelling, we, like she, would simply melt. In this issue of Five Fingers Review *the editors examine the nature of skin and what lies beneath it, and the writings they have selected reveal, ultimately, discoveries of self and soul in all its complexity. For as long as the heart pumps, cutting through the skin involves surprise, pain, bleeding, and mystery revealed.*

—*Jaime Robles*

WILLIAM KECKLER

Poem for Laura Riding

Breathing is not nounal
As the dream goes escaping nouns
Spaces where there is the world (created)
Swimming as plant life dissolves
Air into a membrane
This is your language
Skin is thin
Fish breathe through water's membrane
Turning without
Understanding
Under function the essence dissolves
Between meanings
So the plant is not separate
From the image breathing
A thin skin which is sky
Thinking sky
Accessory to essence
The image breathes through function
"A thin straw of dream"
The human interpretation
Seen floating on top, atop reflection
Which is not separate from essence
But a fish swims between images
Concentric ripples
These are water too
Patterns of mind spread
Maybe water
Maybe
Dripping from above, maybe the fish
Are below branches, glassy because wet

Breaking the human surface
Though the plants are wavering in undercurrents
Dreaming images
What is beyond death Is essence
Algal glints like the mind In its currents the mind
The plant holding the fish, an illusion
Meaningless beyond
Moving "deliberate"
Moving as water
Under function the grace
Of images invented not inventing
But breathing
As essence invents
The human which dissolves
Breathing past clarity
Fish poised amid the blooming water-plants
As essence
What is seized instantly
Under the roots of image
Phanerozoic time
Archaic time
Time before humans, imaged
Erroneously
As time, which is not yet function
The fish turn through dark and light
Turn through light and light
As a sort of scripture
Is useless
To the turning light
Fish move through images
Turn through light and light
The weighing of two essences
Through dark and dark
Between pages between breathings
Between meanings there is a snare

A catch
A lens
Larval as the dream, spinning
Spinning with invention its own clarity
Posing as essence
But what is sealed over instantly
Is time's dream
Is not nounal, is never so
The fish are not nounal
But essence
Past clarity something awakens inside
Swimming
Equivalent with the world (created)
Which dissolves like sky
Fish breathe through
In turning
Eyes emerge as essence
In turning through light and dark
Essence acquires function
Eyes exist
Eyes acquire
Eyes acquire fish
Essence acquires function
Fish through drifting plants (a tropism)
Sleep is this also
Sleep, too, is a fish
Acquiring function through dark and light
The dream is breath swimming
Skin accessory to essence
Images
What goes off in concentric ripples
Like breathing
The consciousness blooming far over
Essence when it's awake
The turning (a tropism)

The human plant
Tendrils, is not perhaps significant
Beyond essence
An open mouth
An open mouth grows the plant of speech
Which is skin according essence
The plant of speech
Which grows past clarity
Into darkness the mouth dips, swimming
The text is water
The text is concentric
Image what goes off, swimming, breathing
The weighing of essence
As certain fish are sleepless
There is only the dream
The eyes of which are larval
Speaking which is separate
Which separates
So scripture emerges without eyes
But concentric images
Images for the ears which listen
Unlike fish which are only eyes
Only vibration
We are these waves
They rush forward, they crescendo
Image a shore
We are these waves
Bearing the thin straw of dream
Across the waves of air
The face is human
Concentric waves of essence
Some call poetry
Some are called
Without function by essence
Which listens

Or there may be concentric listening
As there is concentric speaking
In the aboriginal
This is always realized
But you are not a noun
The act of separation
As close as you'll get to essence
Swimming at the roots, a fish
Lies amid the roots of sound
Is the fish in Sanskrit?
Is the fish in Ur-language?
Tendrils of the eyes please it
As do tendrils of the ear
These please it too
The image floats across the wavering air
The waves are all of time
And concentric
As Sanskrit is in space
Inside many languages the fish
Listens, waits
Your language too (whichever) has a thin skin
Like the sky
Breathing through function its many nouns
You turn under breathing
You turn under seeing
Like the fish
The mind is water, concentric images
Consciousness
Consciousness is other days
Accessory to essence it swims
Distant from language truly
Close to breathing is consciousness
Swimming through plants which are life using sun
Using rhythm
Essence is first, even before fish

There is water-essence
Water-essence imagines fish
It is another language
It is the Word
And the Word is always swimming
Equivalent with the nouns escaping
But there is no first sound

There is essence dividing

And the division was First

April 25: Day of St. Mark, patron of vellum: manufacture and preparation

veinèd day; the daylight through

                           water, water

(and opens the skin)

                  scraped in the sun

    that the words bleed toward

                                 (paper animals of folded milk

    entire translucent herds)

                       to their own reverse

                mirror mirror

    centuries later

soaked in lye for fourteen days   then fourteen again
with the water running

                    over the hand

                  the words spill into

              the framed sun

        of the page

    remembers

in its

        I can see

        through my little skin window

of the mouth of God

        pumiced to glass.

March 8 (Feast Day of John of God, Patron Saint of Printers) 1476: The first Bible printed in Paris

and look now it moves
(just as we knew)   it did & would
                 wherever
you turn
the word of God is a moving thing
whereupon

this act, this one
        times one
        equals
             so what
             ever   you can shift
             at will   will
(they slip)
                    fix
                   at look   at anyone   still
        (be my heart   of
            (as God is to every
clockwork aviary.

Equanimity: The Living Body of Language

The blue hills in the late afternoon November light rolling back
toward the horizon, unreachable, uninhabited, nude. My friend
had said it, the word that would name the hills in this moment,
she said: "remote," and in my eyes the hills throbbed a little,
becoming more of themselves, or at least more apparent to me as
I experienced them. The word, as though arising for the first time,
simultaneously speaking of the hills and the experience of looking
at them in that particular powdery light. "Remote,"
the whole story—title, beginning, middle and end.

The hills backing away cannot be possessed and are as unfathomable
as the mind that suddenly produces the word "remote." In the
moment of lucid seeing the hugeness opens up and one cannot
possess it, either the mind or the object. One's seeing is realized,
the right word floating up like a fragile bubble.

Names automatically used are not the real names, but we use them
as a way to simplify or possess, and in doing so we cut objects off
from their source and make a dead facsimile of the thing.
As Octavio Paz writes in The Monkey Grammarian:
"The poet is not one who names things, but one who discovers that
things do not have a name and that the names that we call them are
not theirs." Writing can obliterate the conventional way of seeing
something so that it can be seen again for the first time.

When the seeing/naming/object arise together there is equanimity
because what is imagined and what is seen are the same.

This unnaming itself participates in the transitory nature of things.
"The conceptions that are the writing are to be disbanded in it,"
writes Leslie Scalapino in her essay, "Silence and Sound/Text."
This is the movement toward equanimity through a language as
volatile as the physical world. Unname the hills with the word

"remote" and they fill the frame of vision while, at the same time, slip away into mist. The works in this section, with their startling images and exchanges, their precision and depth, offer moments of equanimity, as language and subject are so concentrated that there ceases to be a boundary between them.

—Denise Newman

ELIZABETH ROBINSON

Hammock

If a woman were enough preoccupied
with shrinkage

she might have a small child

'Enough' is the sense of it

A mother stutters

The redundancy is tiredness,
could it be made drowsiness

There they are in the bed

The child is a pea under the mattress
they balance so high over

The clasp on a pursing
who sidles out

This is how infinitely small things come to rest

They are not captive, but in relation to enclosure

When the mother sleeps, she has no speech,
but breathes falteringly

Alone, the bed's surface touches
a kind of skin

If the child were to have a mouth, it would be
open, and its eyes partially too aslant

Some erotic fixity of purpose

wh-what is the blanket made of,

how do we hang here

How do I dedicate

the poles to a shrinking pivot

reworded as my son

MEDBH MCGUCKIAN

Photocall

I learned to sing "The Shadow of his Smile,"
swimming through the flooded rooms
of his childhood home. It was the sea
language of a mild, mild day; I discovered
a way of turning from the gold "C"
on his sweater and eleven new faces
watching only me, listening to only me.

I borrowed his arrogance in the make-up
blood, so when I viewed the rushes
there was a single solid red frame
whose eyes belied the most bellicose
hymn to peace. We were dressed for yachting,
in Scotland doubling for China,
neither of us could feel any pain:

but through seven opening doors, the sun
set between our lips moving towards each other
the way the world might die—our requisite
screen kiss like a two-hour Latin Mass
where he matched lips only with the Italian,
pallbearer, boat-maker, ever acted upon,
flower of a dozen dancing lines.

Spring Losses

You walk out from yourself
And at your hands' unangry approach
The cloud laps over the shutter
Wearing my body to nothing.

A river of pleasure runs through
The pipe within my palms
Like a day spent rushing from the house
From those around and within me.

What lay under your touch
Animate as a man standing or a beast
Rising, praised a zero that I stepped beyond
To the day I see thee not.

Locust in the Cemetery

The grave was my favoured post-box,
As difficult as a flower. There was no give
In the fabric of its one-piece floor, walls
And roof, but I slipped into its black
Accent, using his photograph as a fan
Which gave the dark a pedigree of cinnamon
Lashes. My kiss on wood that hollowed
To receive it, was a whisper in the hush
Reflected off the folded blue roses
Bigger than his fist which formed
A silver necklace in the centre, like women
I'd heard laughing while I was growing up.
I laid my body across his
In the shape of a cross, I cut myself
A grave across his head: I took
A meal at the grave by setting
Two vases mouth to mouth in his
Gioconda smile, and then I burned
His body in its tomb and drowned
The burnt bones in honey in a gold
Dish—so when he kisses the drinker
Of this terrifying peace, oblivion
Which is not to be hired
Will be his slave.

Small View of Spire and River

I would be better to sew you a dress with my eye
than to sting your breasts with my tragedies:
five candles breathing without burning for what is yet to come;
I will be glad to find you in the same afterlife.
                                    —BJORNE PETERSEN

The circle that her skirt a brutal red
deliciously brushed created barefoot
on the transdermal earth was my first glorified lips.

A host in white mourning which is said to have bled
was keyed into the solid and correctly treated
moon, as a field writing-desk is built into the top
of a gun-carriage, as a silver-bound pistol
is attached by a ribbon to a little stabbing bodice.

Her inward pulling was an ovary of fire
that sat on the skin of the unmoving world,
carving an embryo on the epistle side,
on the gospel side, to let the next spirit enter,
or let part of the spirit flee.

To protect her low heart from all this patching
and cobbling, she Irished me as the never-sick gods
visit us through illness, and braided this cord
like a felled tree into the mane
of my own child's first pony.

If daylight blessing the land deconsecrated
the gabled home of the sacrament sleeping seated,

or the intervening night only awkward angels
with terrestrial arms were singing
in a mosaic of muses, my soul covered her eyes,
my body paid the sounds she needs to make,
my father's ecstasy and clouds and the immediacy
of mountains in their vertical nativity
were the walls to my mother's ceiling.

the ease after it has been said. the relief of having said it. a
purge. bismillah, let's say. the skin came off without the reluctance
one might have thought. BB says the thrill is gone, gone away for
good. there's some truth in that. thrills can fool the senses.
deceive the pear we call a heart until it becomes an icy pendant.

Something to write until I fall into the sleep of the pillow meisters who insist I use the word meister to signify the spread of my hand from thumb to pinky. When addressing a candle I'm careful to hold in my cough with a Fisherman's Friend in order to not disturb the dust mites in the mattress pad. Here beneath my silky shorts lies a city of lies perspiring at the thought of my dreams that seep through my pillow and form a puddle of banana peels on the floor. The maid will hate me for that. She dyes her hair with ashes from last night's fire and hopes the retarded neighbors don't notice the flames in her part. Why bother with such drivel, dribble, drips. The half moon on my thumb is shining like a carcass, a cow's bones, a thigh to be specific but who asked for specifics or bones or thumbs. If a cow were all thumbs would a dairy farmer laugh himself to death. It's 3 and I think my throat is distilling quantities of silence again. This means I can stop daydreaming about the firehouse and the fireflies from this summer and the fire in my belly that awakens me to cornflakes. My knees can now join in holy matrimony.

I open myself up
to this garbage dump of lava
as it screams out of the hornet's nest
and makes its way to the empty room.
Then I cry the cry of broken trees
as the world goes around
and my body touches ground.

ELÉNA RIVERA

from *Unknowne Land*

"I take it slow"
        Sometimes—
                "What if then *is* now?"

Whether flat or sharp
        I follow the notation
                or perhaps I portent

something else—a descent
        in broad daylight,
                from higher to lower,

if you believe in division,
        a desire for something
                more than an heirloom

at the quivering waterline
        More than my hesitation,
                this shudder at the shore

This meeting of mouths
        trapped with thirst,
                hinged at the surface

Wavering between then
        and now and the rooms that fit
                inside me like columns

Where is the door to this one
        or that one? I watch light
                steal under water

so that it ripples,
    so that snow will melt
        from previously forgotten

silenced or deadened parts
    of the body—the pull of the line,
        as fibers twist and coil

around the corner of my past
    How can I know the present
        if the swollen cry "Restrain"?

"Excessive!" "Demanding!" "Too . . . !"
    Those tugs on the leash
        that bled the engram,

that decimated the floorboards,
    that filled the drawer with water
        so that there wouldn't be enough

room remaining, or else flushed
    down the pipes, the impurities
        filtered, and a life force depleted

At the intersection of two
    roads, be not bound by
        cultivation, by exact

measurements; this kind of
    oblivion will cramp and fetter
        the spirit, this "fitting in"

What have we managed to
    change but the surface?
        Nuances. Words used to describe

"Too!" I hear an echo of it
    in my ear, a legacy
        passed on so that I was

split and divided—but I want to
    descend along the dense,
        animate river encircling the earth

I want to glide softly over
    the cold ocean like a Monarch
        butterfly, plunge into its opacity

But I am stopped short—
    gasping, grasping, barely
        a breath in all my. . .

A mort is heard in the
    distance—a killing is made
        in overwhelming quantities

Minnows balance themselves
    "and the sudden silent trout
        all lit up, hanging,

trembling"   Traveling
    in a felucca through
        a shade called "America"

A past cut in bone
    What's in a name?
        A cascade? An ideogram?

An emblem? And beneath it?
    Dominion is devoid of light
        Can't even swim across the moat

GEORGE ALBON

from *Fire Break*

Does the sky disrupt? I followed you, you were rapid, I followed you to seal it off. The horse's head grew long so that the eyes would rise above the grass line, to notice predators. The sidelong glance grew so inscrutable I really felt I was in another world. They seemed all live things with hearts in them. My palms are out, their symbols of that are patent. *Don't* go crazy—I need more time to fold in the last time, the signature in black crayon taking up the middle of the page. I would love to hop in such a way that it would communicate to sparrows, subtitles at the grass line. Tropical environs conceals that this is the United States, the "help" live here not affording the mainland. The amnesiac way the help live at the edge. I sought your knee during the presentation, its hairiness like a horse blanket. Such that a cloud cover would also seal off while it augured. Sweat on the surface, your new expression, my liquid need. The whisper curls. The sky disrupts.

Movement of honey down the wall,
because like the sun after

contact with the hill

behind which it moves down

so that you can watch it, it's time

or that described by "some
thing," then to witness
that time happening in
an exact correspondence, honey / time

sun-hill / time   what I am

being where, and then, then
a fluent resolve might be uncovered

A solid white billboard above the A-frame,
between large messages

Ocean bed in the open air,
ice   magnetism

where the continent sloughs away
my destiny in the re-telling

launched without motive,
a pencil rolling off

Man migrated to watcher
as his lawn dropped

Speed invented in the face
of a massive horizontal

the uneven cauldron of all signs,
even the arrows: mystery.

I live in the ladle's
abrupt upbringing   folded leaf

the pure city at one end,
burned city, the other's,

what it means   what it does
to drive one's stake

into the loosening fiber,
alive   somewhere above the X.

ELIZABETH WILLIS

Van Tromp, Going About to Please his Masters, Ships a Sea, Getting a Good Wetting

after J. M. W. Turner

Constancy scribbles itself out in waves: a revisionary litter of brown light. Fleety with anchor and going abroad, a fulcrum pulls to left of center. A slap in the face of a sail. A device spies down a-swing in salt & gunpowder, an amber passage. Horizons cast their calm tunes. It doesn't take a traitor to overturn a boat. It wouldn't take such amber to blue up the sky. A heavy craft in wordy water, taking on a master. Van Tromp at the prow, asunder surrounded, clothes himself and sets the sail to follow out his inner course. What is his fiction to the boot of manacles, what is I to the future of pain, of boy, of boat life. Afield and legion. The opposite of grass.

The Heart of Another Is a Dark Forest

after Ford Madox Ford

Believing in my velvet way, I feel the urn to fall dearly. An ancient light crushing the heavy breath of Man. A siege or shadow to follow. I am but a child on a carpet, a democrat called to account for my thoughts. What more can I hope for than to one day be the subject of a really good paragraph in a great man's book? Rossetti "the great man," and everything else is woman. She of the elaborate mind, who elevates the evening with a subtle tart. A crystal palace for baking.

Two Girls with Oleander

after Gustav Klimt

Two girls beneath
an olive and a rose:
a poisonous honey
a hidden elocution
upon a classical ranch
I dare your poem to be
as rhododendrous
as sweet, I dare its
neck to be long, its
origin African
its movement Indian
I dare such velvet
tendonous curls
to grow in a garden
between Egypt and Rome
A letter that crosses
a face in a pediment
a city of music
mere figure, mere scent

Constable's Day Off

Loving the human bird—
the bright converse
of yellow-flowered grasses—
why aren't we lying
in miles of weedy clover?
The bright boat, tumbling through it
the blue of it—Or,
taking the kid out of the picture
(what you loved to see)
a girl who talks to birds—Don't go
Let's delay or—like Shakespeare—"fly"
all disappointment
in the green and untidy
molecular air

CYDNEY CHADWICK

Holiday

She resolves to be cheerful, but cues up a c.d. of Bach's Cello Suites, which would make the most buoyant person mournful. Concerto number four drifts into the bathroom as she stands putting on makeup. When she finishes, fatigue creeps into her body, her brain. She's only been awake for an hour, so will not allow herself to be tired. The woman applies a finishing touch of lipstick. She is fairly certain wearing makeup makes it easier to face the world.

The woman drives to her office to finish up some pre-holiday details. She dials information for a telephone number. The information operator gives her the wrong one—for a meat packing plant in Mississippi. When she calls again to request the charge be removed, it seems to cause a great deal of confusion and annoyance on the part of the present operator. At the end of the discussion she is fairly certain the charge will appear on her statement—at least once.

She must also send some information to a company, and calls the receptionist for the e-mail address and fax number. The e-mail bounces almost immediately, and after she writes out a fax the company's fax machine rings and rings without making any connection. When she calls to recheck the number, there is a recorded message saying the office will reopen on January 3rd.

The woman remembers a time, not all that long ago, when the numbers she requested were correct, when packages arrived at their appropriate destinations, when telephone calls, faxes and other communications elicited responses and when it didn't require doing a task several times in order to get results.

o

It is a well-established fact that people become more psychologically unbalanced at this time of year and her car is almost hit by several sport utility vehicles on her way downtown.

42

In several shops the woman buys last-minute gifts and stands in line to have them wrapped. She hopes they are the right books, that it is the ultimate sweater, and if not, that these items will not be completely useless or offensive to the recipients.

At the market while buying the usual holiday accoutrements, sweets and fattening food, a store clerk crashes a dolly loaded with cases of wine into her ankle. He responds with an indifferent *sorry*, and leaves her hopping toward the breads.

Out in the parking lot she finds she is blocked in by someone who is double-parked, dumps her groceries in the back seat and honks the horn. Customers glare at her as they enter the store. No one comes to move the car, so while honking and waiting, the woman pulls a pear from one of the grocery bags and begins to eat. For the first part of the season she has found herself absently putting food into her mouth and now feels uncomfortably expanded, as if her body were a damp sponge.

A man in rotting clothing who has left a Salvation Army storefront crosses the parking lot swearing loudly: fuckin' bastards. It's Christmas and they still won't give me a coat! They talk about *rules*. Jesus never had any rules. He only had *suggestions*. The man sees her looking at him and shouts at her through the rolled up car window: can't even have a drink with Christmas dinner at the shelter. No money, they treat you like a little kid. He wanders off without even asking for change.

The pear isn't enough. Shortly after eating it she is more hungry than she was before. She would like to fill her stomach and sleep under a thick blanket until sometime in the new year.

o

That evening the woman's boyfriend calls and she can tell he's been drinking. He suggests they break up, but after talking nonstop for another fifteen minutes, says perhaps they should get married. She isn't sure if he is proposing, decides that is something she does not want to think about just now.

o

43

On Christmas the family decides to be hyper-convivial, which makes for a hysterical tension lying below their every move and word.

The woman has a hard time discerning if anyone likes the gifts she has gotten them—or not—if the oohs and aahs are imitation oohs and aahs.

Around the table some pick up the thread of an argument begun the year before, perhaps unconsciously, for they all know how to upset and annoy one another—or they just can't help themselves. A cousin seated next to the woman covertly discusses with another cousin how her father would have preferred a daughter like that—indicating with her knife a woman toward the head of the table, another cousin's second wife. She is thin, with hair curled by a curling iron; she smiles at everyone and seems to be eating only vegetables. The whispering cousin suddenly throws her knife onto her plate and leaves the table to go outside and smoke a cigarette.

At the other end of the table a nephew takes an entire platter of appetizers in one of his large hands, dishes mini-quiches into his plate and monopolizes the conversation, saying things like it is wrong to stage a war and bomb innocent people to retain political power. He seems to think his superior mental powers have drawn him to this conclusion before anyone else.

An aunt rolls her eyes at a brother-in-law's tie adorned with hot air balloons, a gift, undoubtedly, from one of his children—while a father eats with rapid bites, hunched and concentrated on his plate, like someone is lurking behind his chair waiting to whisk away his meal if he were to pause.

They gather in the living room for the after-Christmas-dinner movie, a comedy that should offend no one. During the film, which doesn't hold the woman's interest, she reads a magazine article stating that aging is the result of damaged cells caused by free radicals roaming loose in the body. Free-radicals are formed by eating unhealthy food, alcohol, pollution and other environmental factors. It explains that cells succumb to oxidation—the same process that causes wine to spoil, butter to turn rancid, paint to chip and peel away.

She can feel the blood pounding in her temples and wonders if her blood pressure has been raised by the Christmas food and the family— which seems like a meta-family she is now engulfed in without a self.

That night as the woman tries to sleep in a guest room, she lies awake hearing sounds she is unused to—doors slamming, wind blowing through wooden shutters, a toilet flushing in another part of the house.

In her worst moments she thinks all her life consists of is going from menstrual cycle to menstrual cycle—as when older it will be going from pension check to pension check. *Cheerful,* she admonishes herself and rolls over in the bed.

The following day she stops for breakfast on the road and indulges herself in an omelette, potatoes and lots of strong coffee. She feels depleted, weak. The smell of a grill, the flowered curtains and waitress uniforms are reassuring. She wonders if she and her boyfriend will continue. Ever since Thanksgiving their disagreements, sarcasms and hurt feelings have escalated to another level, and lurk like phantoms behind their current conduct and words.

Back in the city she decides to run a few errands before returning to her apartment, which will be cold, since before leaving she turned the heat down to save money.

The people she encounters in the post office, in the store that sells high quality coffee and teas, at the shoe shop with a post-Christmas 50% off, are dazed, bewildered. There is a considerable lag time before they answer questions or ring cash registers.

When the woman arrives home, she turns up the heat, puts away her purchases and turns on the c.d. player. She forgot to remove the last disc so the familiar music once again floats through the apartment. It seems different today, wistful rather than melancholy.

She calls several people who remained in the city for the holiday. Some she leaves messages for, but those she speaks to are also distracted and unable to concentrate.

She has time on her hands and doesn't know what to do.

Everyone behaves as if they have been away for a long time, and have just returned, weary and blinking, from a vivid yet peculiar country.

She sits on the couch and imagines she must be comporting herself in the same way, but being in and of herself, ensconced in a body, inhabiting a brain—with cognition occurring and synapses firing, she cannot get far enough away from herself to know.

Perhaps those she saw over the last twenty-four hours had, in turn, scrutinized her—although she finds this somewhat unlikely, as most seemed to place their attention elsewhere. Nonetheless, she toys with the idea that they, too, were observing and deducing. If she made an impression, she speculates on its duration: a minute, longer? She wonders if the notion *had* gone beyond "relative," or "customer?"—and if the surveillance had gone deeper, did the thoughts run along the lines of: "Here is someone I believe I know well, because we are blood." Or, "This person appears demure—I do not need to prepare myself for unpleasantness and diffficulty." She reflects on the amount of time she might have existed in their consciousness, how long they had hovered about in hers.

As she sits on the couch halfway listening to a Bach cello concerto, she has the feeling she is being watched. It could be the smug owner of a new telescope, a gift from the previous day, or it might be a thin man framed behind window panes. Someone could even be perceiving her as she is at this moment seeing herself—a small thing in a smallish room, an entity caught up in a prodigious and complex scheme she never agreed to be in, and which in spite of all the eyes and vocabularies, continues to elude them all.

ALICE JONES

Verbs

Open

What we have in hand is a bunch of questions. Don't pander to common sense. We're beyond that, not that it's pandemonium we're after; it's just—be Pandora—open the box—there might be hell or the next pandemic, there might be a panda lazily chewing her bamboo, maybe Pindar penning odes (if they had pens then), or the grand panjandrum telling us what's what. Stand still, don't push the panic button, just look.

Halt

Surprised, rounding the corner, to see a peacock running down The Alameda, tail furled, stopping traffic with his presence. Some forms of matter never enter other phases naturally, stay gas or liquid unless you take them down, approaching absolute zero, which you never get to. Lying on our new deck, looking up at stars, I thought your breathing stopped. One drop of olive oil hanging, held there, on the bowl's glass lip. Wondering what it meant, the lame, the halt, the blind . . .

Know

Science is the scion of seeing. Darwin worked it out: the sequence of lumpy turtles, bumpy iguanas, penguins, in the Galápagos, a zion of creatures who unbecame, sighted with a sigh, hence our map of species, divided by the scimitar of time, each one a sequin in the eye of what we know.

Conceal

Not writing. A dress without a belt. The locked drawer. Henna. Passing. The bedroom door. "There is no gold buried here." A bottle hidden in the bottom of a trash bag. Landmines. The closet. The stash. Veil. Turtle shell, black tights, witness relocation, the Klan's hood, masquerade. I didn't want you to know. Allure: come find me.

Augur

A knotty question. We ought to trace an answer. You know tea and its leaves. I want ground coffee, not tea. Naughty boy, gnawing the teething ring, clear through. It's coming: the year ought-ought. Increasing awe. Now tease me again.

ANDREW LINDSAY

The Peanut Man

I never wanted to be The Peanut Man. I made that clear at the start, I begged and pleaded. But the Reverend Father is a hard, harsh man, he said it was my sacred duty of atonement, that I must be The Peanut Man. He said it's as I've sinned—that's true enough, and being The Peanut Man's a way to get some peace of mind. But it's a rotten job.

You have to run the gauntlet of every child in the parish—we're good breeders, there's easily one hundred kids. You have to run dressed as The Peanut Man, with a sack over your eyes and a suit of sackcloth too, it's on the sackcloth suit are sewn peanuts.

The children run at you to pluck the peanuts off. The trouble is they get a kind of peanut frenzy into them. You can see it in the way they set their mouth, it's poking out but then it's hard, it's set and doesn't move, not like a mouth with lips—that flesh was made to move, as when we speak or kiss, it's supple flesh. But no, these children's mouths set hard, set on one thing, they want to get The Peanut Man.

It's not enough for them to get the peanut off, somehow the Peanut Man takes a greater sense for them. He is the symbol of denial, of all the pleasure withheld right through the year, all the good things out of reach, all the tenderness they craved perhaps from kin that's been denied. And all the strange emotions this evokes.

They get that hard look in the eye, that's when the soft skin of the mouth begins to set. The Peanut Man! They want revenge. They want revenge for all the crimes they feel the adults have committed against them. It's a childish rage, perhaps, but there's a mighty anger in a child's closed fist. The Peanut Man! That's me. I'm running through the glade, the Reverend Father bid me so, it is my penance, the children's fists close first around a peanut on my suit, that's how the fist is formed, and then they pluck. Perhaps they pluck away one sin, but then somehow they always punch with their compact peanut fists, a peanut punch into the back or front or sides of The Peanut Man.

The little bastards mean to kill me, that's for sure. Suffer the little inno-cents to come unto me. A child is never innocent. Look into their eyes at birth and see a thousand years of sorrow, a thousand years and more. The little bastards, born with such cruel knowledge in their eyes.

And what will happen when the peanuts have run out? They'll stone me then, club me to death, or push me over a cliff? Perhaps that's what the Reverend Father meant when he said, It's good for you! A divine act, a kind of salvation. Perhaps he meant—I see it now—this is my chance to be a martyr, fallen at the hands of the children of our village. A Picnic Martyr, that's what I am.

There'll never be another picnic, not without me, The Peanut Man. Or if there is, it will be black and sombre, a dark affair, the shadow of my death hanging over everyone like those great black clouds that let down thunderclap and rain. That's it to be, for sure, no turning. It's a curious kind of destiny, to be The Peanut Man.

GIGI JANCHANG

A Description of Two Installations: Cross Your Eyes and Blue Eyes

"Cross Your Eyes" is an installation covering two rooms. In the first room, two eight-foot-long fluorescent lights are mounted about twelve feet apart—one is vertical and placed close to the entrance, and the other is horizontal, positioned farther back on the ceiling. When walking into the room one perceives the two lights coming closer and closer to each other. What the spectators don't realize is that at a certain vantage point the two lights form a reflection of a cross in their eyes.

In the second room there are displayed nearly one hundred photographs of eyes with crosses reflected in them. The photos help people realize what took place in the first room, thus altering their perception of the installation and creating a desire to match their imagination with their actual sight.

In the second installation, "Blue Eyes," a photographic color portrait completely covers a six-by-six-foot window. The irises of this portrait are cut out to make the exterior scene shine through. This installation includes indoor lights which complement the outdoor light and consequently render the eyes blue.

At a distance, the image is perceived as two-dimensional. As one approaches the portrait, the scene through the holes gradually appears to be three-dimensional. The difference between reality and a photographic matter becomes clearly distinguishable.

Media plays a major role in most people's lives, and as the dependence on technology increases, representation begins to substitute for reality and seeing becomes less important. Is what we think, believe, and imagine in balance with what we see? Is there a way to expand our capacity to reflect through open eyes? These are the issues that I investigate in my installations.

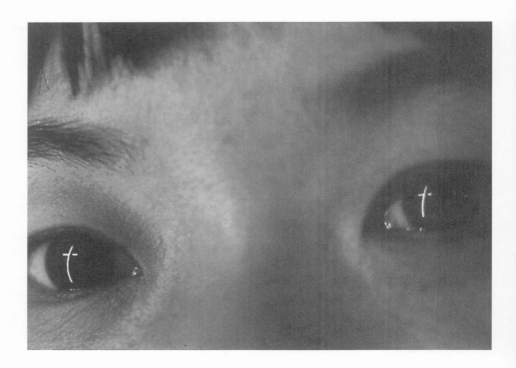

GIGI JANCHANG, ABOVE: *Cross Your Eyes,* installation, two 8' fluorescent lights, overall
10'x 12'x 12', 1989
RIGHT: *Blue Eyes,* installation, color photograph, 6'x 6', 1995

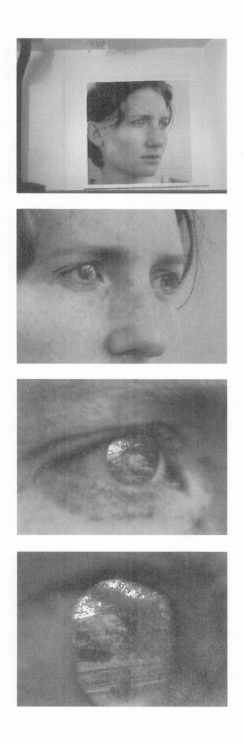

GEORGE KALAMARAS

Improvisation

Language, like tongue, is not sound litmus cannot in lethargy, that is, pin an owl's photons to the tentative hairs on your chest

Sounds from across the room drift by like uncollected smoke, or dust particles of thought almost come together finish book, parrot pie, glossary that sink, wash clothes, free lunch, eleventh muse

Words, she said, are words are only you're crazy she said you're

What about the comma's pearl gives pause when breath seeps out into the dying, when rests become, when desires to roam the streets like an insolent buffalo disoriented in downtown Boise

    Don Byrd, Charlie Parker, Bob Barker

She played a saxophone right there on network t.v. I could almost said I could almost feel her heat saying, *love me, baby, am I real?*

    Charlie Byrd, Don Barker, Bob Parker

What is left unsaid lies about us like an unwanted organ, like the silk tiger of nightsweats, a gold hoop designed for a hidden ear, liver stains on a clay coffee mug, a thirteenth rib luminous and soaked in potassium sulfide

There was a there was an explosion my ears felt it in the curving of a peapod, in the damp sheets, in the hairy palm of growing up and up and something in tasting the color orange when watching her bathe in blue origami aquarium light, while aster cranes, dark silty riverous thread

Li Po, in dropping the moon's dirge, in dress in the midnight magnolia
silent delicate vowel of a geisha chewing straw

One words down a noisy worm into the dark molecular leaves of it, a
black cord bobbing from the navel like a manic sea urchin, a sound without mouth a word without meaning, like a soft encrustation losing its fix,
like a song with no sock, music moist, she heard her fingers say in the
skeletal dark, the ribs split and watery and nasaly and roots

   Bob Byrd, Charlie Barker, Blue Tourniquit Air

Parking your breath in the sex of a fern brings all manner of embarrass-
ment. The face goes red. Your nest flushes. The hairs on your chest
sprout dreadlocks, like new shoots of a spider plant, like a boy with five
creamy palms. Like an insomniatic fluid counting backwards to one. The
amoeba in your pie fills with fruit. The paramecia in your sock. The food
in your parrot. And, oh, the saw in your stew. You see a musician on the
street, and the minnow holes in your ribs suddenly expand. You grow a
fondness for salt

Somebody blows a blues in flute peacock light, in the watery reeds of
your hair, in the under water underside, in the slow deliberate of speech,
in the *mantras* of dust. Somebody, that is, turns over a feather for a
tongue, says *yes* with a gesture of goldfish, says *yes* in turns of liquid bees,
in the silver plate, in the collections of sound advice is a limp, is the slow
slip of dark, the breaking apart of syntax can't and never will but won't.
You taste her fluid and spacious weight, you face her syllabic steep, and
you want to wash the dog, walk the car, soften the cud, anything remotely stable remotely standard any regularly vowel, you want to, yes,
soak it in spinach, you want to cough it up once and for, you want it like
money, like a cup of green hair, like a teaspoon of black morning pepper,
you want to get the saliva just right

AJA COUCHOIS DUNCAN

Skin and Its Appendages
from *Taxidermy*

her body, gathered wilderness

under canvas

marooned

in strata   corium

another labyrinth of stitches, tracks splaying the knot of abdomen
each breast burrowing her veins a rushing train the hiss of air and metal
a brutal motion or no motion at all as if stillness is the aberration,
thought—the noise she cannot bear

the faint percussive beat   swollen   sound filtered through

blood an ocean without the glamour of the moon or stars only dark
and motion and the fibrous bands closely reticulated disposed

on the nature of skin the area measured volume in cubic feet the density of fat cells sinew molten

muscle constricting the isolated follicle the capillaries deliberate breaks toward the surface the striations of dark and light a maze of hair and black moles the utter expanse of limbs aching for blood or suffering her body painfully exposed clammy the layers of spheroidal cells shedding impossibly new

sub-cutaneous

> night, not dark
> but iridescent
> fish gleaming
> the thick liquid

> her heart

or ours together, stitched
the tendons, a compound hinge
swings shut, the unknown
arteries or ducts flooded

> brilliant, the darkness
> our open mouths
> approximating the aching maw

no matter what is severed from the body
there is no loss of pressure
the heft of bones

                  as dead shudder from our weight
                  muffled by dirt, the pitch of grass

our burden, the pull of skin
brittle bones   our wrists
ankles so narrow   snap

torn through

on the absence of skin, the flesh exposed, calcified, her eyes or fear
stripped down to a singular particle

ghosts   marrow filling each vessel of bone

the burned, dismembered, bound by their own entrails, cities cleared

down to the gums, the dark fascia laced with fat and nerves

her eyes, fear, terminal filaments recoiling

                              witness, not a sound but a mark
        a blemish, the raised surface, smooth, hairless
                a scar traversing the horizon
                        corpus   furrowing red earth

LUKE TRENT

What Comes Together

In bodies that warm tongue

keeps tinder with an 'e' Verbs

crack open; conversation's

on a leash, animals raised by

eyebrows. Every slow thing

is magic turning circles over

ears and skin; in acts a

kind of hope cutting through

walls and pithy aneurysms

embedded in rhythms

that carries music back inside.

Poem Not Your Master's Chamber

        The hurry to go
where feelings come to make
    the same

    Lovely adverbs lovely salad,
sound

        (hOLES)
                'balls of the
                paté'

            E   E
    The W 'n' Y   (in
            E   E   theory)

    infused

            —but split off—
each thumb's
                equivalent

            (moon)
one hand's differing motion

    to honesty, whore & muse

The Deep as Good

Uncertainty spiders, her blue mirror & "tawdry
Heaven." Therefore's forever loose behind Comma's

doozy migraine. She's olive, Miss Modesto, irises'
flattened penny, breast sunflowers by a cotton

field; memory's bicycle's made of skin, dresses
wet-clipped to tight lines across the lightwell.

Now, whenever another crazy, golden mango weaves
the rabid eyeteeth, her slow-glistening "mouse

in an empty boat" glides out from under tongue.

Prix Fixe

Name's nothing
you will surprise me
with

Years spent driving
without radio   (whisper)

of sober teachers

—At first the glue
tasted good slowly
swallowed

Little Pete there,
chortling pakeha

The only one who knew

                    ○

(The future begins in the
        same voice)

            A spiral
& these fragile annuals,
                        purple
& yellow hills.

Orange road workers
bloom in dry grass after rain's
unhemmed cement

so they're needed.

    Some Bighead in a jeep

       don't they always

          o

    Calls you answer you answer
immediately   (Don't

write letters)

       Everything's Fine

          o

Her last evening's left

message (wishing well) though pride-

ful & karma-loaded. Reminiscing

that first trip North, chilly

frittatas, bed springs listing,

sweat-silkened hours of talk—

Dali's pointed grin the bottom of

each hot chocolate.

o

A volume of blood nobody counts on...

Misperception's magic

                    . Everything
curled like Elphaba's green legs under
Dorothy's house

   rarely suffices

          Small red potatoes
          baked with olive oil and finished
          with glaze of satay

"I hear they've split ..."

          Hazelnut pancakes
          with light yoghurt
          and hazelnuts, blue and black-
          berries, juice

"She hasn't really missed him ..."

          Oysters (half shell) orange-
          tomato soup, local fruit
          sorbets

"She does better without him ..."

          Venison in red wine dijon
          sauce, leafy salad.

Ambivalent Guest

Apart from acting as a protective cover or layer for that which it contains or as a means of identification (the color of), skin serves as a boundary between an interior and an exterior, something that must be passed through. I find this notion of passage compelling, as it creates a third place (between departure and arrival) from which to negotiate being. I want to push the metaphor of skin as a passageway out of the physical body and into the social world, to explore the possibilities of skin as a corridor between places, languages, or events, or as an interval between what is known and unknown, desired and met.

With the corridor in mind, the next step is to interject a person into the transitory space. What happens to the subject there? I imagine: "A person stands outside a door, facing the door, uncertain about entering. Outside of this door there is a hallway, in which the person stands. On the other side is a room where the person may or may not want to be." The ambivalence of travel and the multitude of states one occupies while traveling strike me. In a culture so focused on arrival and assimilation, one can forget to consider the hesitancy of the person in the hall, the resistance. The hall, in this case, is the city, the nation, relations between people (be they lovers or strangers), speech, and the imagination.

The ambivalence of putting forth, of showing up, of existing within or without, and of revealing one's self, permeates each of the works in this section. Through this theme, the writers and artist explore not only varied aspects of social alienation or habitation, but also a self-conscious crossing of worlds, time, and relations.

—*Renee Gladman*

WILL ALEXANDER

from *The Sri Lankran Loxodrome*

. . . according to the voice
to the apparition Gianini
I am spectral
vampiric
with my voice always lingering in the waves
& I hypnotize the waves
& make the monsters flow backward

perhaps a sum of damaged engenderments
or because
of my volatile teleportation
here are depths which I ignite
which include the labroid fishes with their throat teeth
with their "protrusile Jaws"
with their continuous dorsal fins
or perhaps a "Batfish"
or a "Peacock Flounder"
but I am perfected on the "Order Squamata"
the "Family" Hydrophidae
closely related to cobras
neurotoxic
hypnopompic
viperous

they tend to "shun the deep sea"
& so I snare them at certain moments
& filter their "drop for drop" venom through my optic nerves
this is why Gianini includes me as a specter
as a loiterer in the reefs
& I reply to this ghost
that I am gorgonian in density

that I arrived on this earth from the holocaust of being
that I had no "gill slits"
no "labial furrow"
that I was capable of speaking of a glossary of ferns
or of a zone of radiolarians
or of a moon of Spotted Goat fish
with its flickering anatomy
destined for Telesto
or Umbriel
Or Larissa

for me
the sun expands in the water
like a burning half-dated carbon
like a space of neutral raylets
where solar mass is quickened
where ratios project & divide
because each underwater wind is a negated Vulturnus
like a force conceived through linguistic prosecution
beyond any factor sufficient to it
by which
I lower my atomic hebetics
so as to challenge the utter sourness of "Hydrophidae"
so as to swallow the bacteria of their nuclei
so as to contact swans at another level of existence in early Kemet
understanding in essence the quadrants of Venus
the ripening horses on Calypso
the listless wars ensuing on Iapetus & Pandora
wars concerning "Bolometric luminosity"
because
as I utter to Gianini that biomedicinal waters need weight
need their scorpion chatter to produce power
in the form of brightened interior crows
like a forge giving gold from a manger
from which dwarfs

from which Sandworm nerves
become of uttermost potential
which presents a toleration beyond human acquisition

let me say
that I solemnly know the pteropods
the blue shelves of fauna
the caliginous glow of the continental slopes
which plummet with shocking spells of charisma
at a depth minus abstract immobility
minus deployed compression
minus the realm which identifies the "thermocline"
at which the slope steeply rivets
"100 miles . . . downward"

there then exists a magnetic stellar blackness
a carnivorous oasis of blackness
where the suns derive their power from obscurity
from the oceanic trenches
producing in my mind a forceful Kodiak crustacean
or an invisible kelp dragon

Gianini whispers from the void
that my mind is unconditionally slanted
that the monsoons have obscured my skull with treason
that my darkness exists beyond alchemical proportion
knowing that I possess the constant interpretation of
crimson explorational hamlets
at the strata of the Benthic
at the dark undoing of metric differential

again Gianini hovers as he whispers
that my face is glass
that my eyes are demoralized
that my temperature is deprived like an Auk

that I've reduced the fiery glow of Eistla Regio
that the tense Venusian summers cannot hold me

no
I do not dwell at the height of a necessitous nervous focus
so I listen at the level of the biometric gulfs
stretching conditions to a taut definition in English
as to what drowned land conditions might obscure
or a fully developed fish expiring in torment
akin to a maze in a turbulent Crimea
like a trait of desolation

& there are days when I claim mirages as my fate
when I smell error in the way the sea explodes
when the magnesium gates are dissolved
as I sail above the Amsterdam Fracture
or the Gascoyne Plain
or finding myself blowing through the Mozambique Channel
& near the south flow exists a counter-clockwise motion
& near Sri Lanka the opposite motion transpires

I call the monsoons hermits
at other times they earn the appellation of colloquial straw
because the northern current reverses
& I am reduced to intoning at the depth of the Java Trench
because Gianini knows there are only snakes to catch
only snakes to populate the trawler
with its somnific flask
with its verdurous weathering
with its shape of an eel at macrocosmic twilight

Gianini whispers
that I eat Spartina grass
that I indulge in "invertebrate chordates"
that I drunken myself on a cunning hydroid liquor

you see
Gianini relates to Sri Lankan minerals
mentally feeding on graphites & gems
he whispers that he hails from Jaffna
& I hail from the eastern shore where we dance the Kaferingha
I feel as though evolving from a sphere
which exists as diaphanous clepsydras
a republic of ambrosia
brought to its power
by the fact of anesthesia
so that the Indian Sea
with its transitional flux
with its analogy between life & death
allows me the complication of a smoking sea urchin's vortex
certainly not a pasture of bullocks
or the zodiacal life marked by exterior scale
or the mathematical ingestion of a squid

& I am not speaking of skioptic "response"
which relates
only to "light and shade"
or to a primitive form of shadow

it is not that I am a bloodless form
full of scarification & heat
or
aborted & microplanchic

I have a burning love of verbs
a driven micro-sorcery
alive
within a blank hellish drone
as a ghostly cheval
staying alive by crucifying prudence with my compass
my body being of dark electrical thorns

like a watery desert of deserted veins
fishing for serpents
embroiled by Gamma Cygni
a "white supergiant 800 light years away"

it enhances grace
it spins the body in physical movement
like a stunning kind of pictograph
above my "Intrapsychic conflict"
I am never within the structure of jealousy or depression
electrically hidden in massless ice sheets
more
like an evasive expansivity
an expansion unblemished by the cubic or by volume

it is above galactic latitude
like a lepton fountain
dispersed by geocentric parallax
by a simple dwarfing containment

perhaps I am more condoned
by the "Hirayama" family of asteroids
that I have broken with human motion
in that the cells are collected & dispersed

collected on the level of the prone visible body
then dispersed on a plane much higher than neutrinos
true
the galaxy cosmologically shifts
leaving me deranged at the psychic diametric of velocity
an ulterior body whose passing is "short lived"

in this fundamental sense
I am Mahayana & of Africa
both Sri Lankan & non Sri Lankan

in that
I am of a newly elected "Radial" width
comprehending my projection of rays
like faceless chromium at twilight
an absence
like "intergalactic hydrogen"
perhaps a complex love of gravitons & lightning

I learned to speak when my solar journal was commenced
then I was magnetized at the age of 12 to a fleeting form
of fatherhood
& now I sail
never eating for days consumed by scalar neutrinos

I've been reported as expired in Jaffna
& been burned in effigy for interminable wandering
for the crime of emitting vertigo by my movement
for inflicting the human spirit with a parallel genetic
engenderment
being compared to the sun in the afterlife

a wanderer in a zone with fluctuating kelvins
breathing unknown dice within my schisms

at times I swallow peril & Gianini teleports to Jaffna
& scorns me
returns to the trawler like ghost
to mock me
to fulminate my captures
to heap upon my cells a code of abrasive torment
threatening to pile up scholars at the behest
of my eternal disadvantage
their argument being
that the winds will one day dissipate
that my oxygen will flare out like a nova

incoherent in demise
that the "Gulf of Mannar" will disappear
that I'll return to realize no proper distance can quantify
& so I ask of Gianini
did the Buddha ever waver?
did he cease to exist because of unjust reason?

Gianini then disappears & disappears
remaining sequestered in a liminal Jaffna
in a turquoise incompleteness
making his way through insidious salamander flowers

as for me
the shock
the uncompromising totalitarian sky
muttering in a lake of connivance
de-configured by maggots
there then exist for me
durations of time
of deadly sojourns in circles
transfixed in planktonic oblivion

& so there exists nothing as outward circumstance
as separated boundary
as immaculate bell to be rung without the core of
aboriginal timing

so I exist
without the ultimatum
without the creatureless blackness that the preachers pursue

I am without didactic conundrum
without the law which inverts & shatters
& invents the cold incontrovertible monuments
which contort & psychically poison

the neural field then subject to bloodless catastrophe
to a range within distorted phrenic reality

me
I'm condemned to tragic imperceptibles
to cauterized anomalies
open at a depth of wandering enigma
which exists at maniacal apogee
incapable of termination
or the magical shapes in sun enriched snowlight
so Gianini has become a traitor who ferociously exists
who dwells at Guénonian blazeless incandescence
as a poltergeist capable of terminal teleportation
like: a witness within a graph of integers
watching me
chop off the head of a serpent
with my rusty spade
with my hands like magic lightning hooks
from the beginning of this strange vestibular Journey
casting spells
which combine & supercede the galaxies
like the shadow from a dying igneous torrent

because I have never sought in my wandering
a catechismic plankton
or a global dossier on movement
I can only reveal to one
the structure of magnets
& the way charisma ignites above a zodiac of disfavour

so I am never annulled
or pillaged by disfiguring darkness

when Sri Lanka floods
I am empty
transparent without resistance

condoning the power of its valence
refusing to keep a log
or handle a rapacious coding journal
so that Odysseus or Marco Polo exist without analogy
or profit to my mnemology

for instance
the moon as conundrum for millipedes
for jolts of interminable stillness

so what the mind would call confrontment
what the reductive mental faculty would deem as equational fear
no longer dissolves me
no longer equates my eternity with phrenic nodels transformed
into prayer
into a mode of dolorous subduction

this is why Gianini appears & disappears spying on my trawler
like a form of arcane treachery
whispering my visage through the highlands into Jaffna
recollecting my shadow as a steep & insidious power
to be negated
to be signed by the ministers from dark judicial hamlets
that I am robbing the ocean of serpents
that my trawler demonically flashes
that I harbor a tribe of sphinxes on board
who've abdicated land
& I
the surviving criminal party
devoid of earthly habitation

neither Sinalese or Tamil
it is said that I hail from Eistla Regio on Venus
that the serpents I catch are forced to imbibe lava

that I'm training non-human forms to invade the Sri Lankan
populace
seeking to steal the root of the land
all this
by one whose name is hidden
who wanders between nothingness & living
who destroys his unnatural cradle by means of unnatural schisms
yet who imbibes as his source general heresy & disjunction

NOTES

Telesto: a moon of Saturn

Umbriel: a moon of Uranus

Larissa: a moon of Neptune

Vulturnus: taken from the Latin adjective *vulturinus,* which is characteristic of
vultures. In this case I have taken license and created a variation on the word
which implies fire or volcanoes

Iapetus & Pandora: moons of Saturn

Bolometric luminosity: ". . . related to the body's surface area and effective temperature . . ." It concerns the luminosity "of a star or other celestial body"

pteropods: ocean dwellers, 1/4" long, have "transparent, papery shells, and are
planktonic"

Benthic: sea bottom

Eistla Regio: volcanic region on Venus

Amsterdam Fracture, Gascoyne Plaid, Mozambique Channel, Java Trench: Geologic
and geographic features condensed within the Indian Ocean

Xaferingha: African-derived dance performed in Sri Lanka

galactic latitude: the angular distance of a celestial body north or south of the
galactic equator

Mirayama asteroids: ". . . debris resulting from a collision between larger asteroids in the past." Named after the Japanese astronomer K. Hirayama

Guénonian blazeless incandescence: ". . . psychic remains left behind by a human
being in passing to another state . . ." as defined by French thinker René
Guénon, who was converted to Islam in 1912, and who died as an "Egyptian
national" in 1951

Jaffna: a city in northern Sri Lanka

giovanni singleton

from *melanin suite*

1st movement

      the study of silence. its evolution a
      guard rail. a corrugated

      tongue. teeth knitted together. silence
      leaves a strain of being work. of looking

      almost dead. shade burns as if to
      interfere. photographs. a need to hold

      still for a moment. everything that
      counts appears in past tense. time

      accumulates as in a reflecting pool.

2nd movement

    stooping in a darkened hallway. salt water
    bodies rock steady. muffled pounding. the
    door of no return. is closed and closer
    and under measured reconstruction. living
    seeps through in echoes. stillness outside
    in. a collective breath persists without
    apology. mud stained spoons undulate from
    shore to distant shore. then one day
    walk as if rowing a boat.

3rd movement

anyone configures everyone at random. long
and short tangents of breath shift then
collide. a departure of selves. memories
and forgetfulness. there in is some predestination. to go on
and into other
spheres. a rear exit. the route made
visible. singularity of purpose breaks
down in momentum. sleep moves without
sound as in amazing grace.

4th movement

we us and thou. the voices. sound a
decidedly downtown destination. the

boulevard. blazing speech. horns blow.
fast and furious. ghostly

drummer makes flight. some rap

tap   tap   tap   tap   tap

conductor of multi-directional live-
wire. crowds gather

behind cranial walls. all smoke-filled.
goat praises. thou. a vast expanse of

skeletal remains. faced down on the
ground as in quilted covering.

giovanni singleton

5th movement

    spinning wheel fortune. stagger the root. warrior

    rifts. a cataclysmic sight. mythical weave of bowed

    heads. discontinuous dreams and drafts. drawing

    hands. acoustic bass. plucked upright. mercurial

    conjure. strings. such tongues ever

    leaning as in revelation.

STEFANI BARBER

from *The Blue Tower*

I

for some she cleans the entire house—
others—just the bedroom
a piece of land too narrow & steep to build
another house on—
in between the 2 that share
the same view as from where

the tiny fenced-in space can be seen
& beyond—the city—which can't
be seen—through these elements

thankful for that—one reality no
one can do anything to effect—
it saves a means of escape

music continues to play in the kitchen—
for no one in particular. they have
argued then made up—an old married couple
she says—tho one is old enough to parent
the other. one asks the other out for drinks
and walks home after work.

thinking—down a hill in this rain.
a lover who knows & is a part of.
second cup of coffee—the day
called for it, and darkened rooms,
and work—how it is defined

2

could be called perfect—if not lonely
return to the same chair at the same table—
bell may have rung or someone
stopped out front

it began to seem constant—always had—
so said to myself—what more could there be—
for example. have always sat here.
have always watched. have never missed.

after a simple wish—what next but the ones
redefined each day—

or also simple if seen from a particular seat
in a particular season—"she's spacing me"

the habit of longing. something was new to me—
then I could not release it—

behind this job—a type of thinking that makes it
matter, makes it worth—what I would
have said—not to look out at the tracks
but to reach—then we'd change differently

at what hour will these conversations
start to be considered "intimate"—
will I be told—not right now—

a harder task than I had imagined
the deductions—the falling into place

3

now she was out—the space she was in—
smelled briefly of a bakery—tho not as warm
a sentry at each door—they watched
for each other—movements were brief—
saying nothing

silencing oneself has the effect—
of an opening perhaps, the kind
sought in places—with names &
histories (the unwritten kind)—
formulas not sufficient for this task—
one might wish for more

as seen from the street—a single
light speaks to numerous—above
where other lights move & are not
stationary—having direction
(what I asked for)   what I will—

an order made, another adhered to
unwillingly, as machines move flesh—
from locations—resisting this
automation, each block ordered—
it seems smaller then—except for
the hills & ghosts of power

"I made it"—"you made it"—
an unexpected collapsing—glass of water
next to the plants—in filtered sun—
then holding, then we started

4

some minutes spent walking thru
the muddy park—the dog who knew
my scent, her owner—whose conversations—
these terms—I bring with me—
not for the first time

for a month he was gone—& his sign
amused the commuters—to pass him
again & not to speak—
to not be one of the girls but
thinking of a need—

a less complicated path—not least
resistance but working—with
what could suggest in this moment—
struggle over these rocks instead—
pause & nod at the driver—
contending with differences—then
taking them places—

why the moods. arriving I would say.
or she would force the greeting—
so I would bend—smile & speak—
overlook what has collected around my feet—
take what was warm—& its meaning

FRED MOTEN

101

the circle laura of agoura
the circle lore my circuit girl
wanna move in your beauty.
this is sad. my transport's no one
else's name like gilmore can't hold
immense blue immense sweet
heavy but that don't work but
the shit is beautiful as if its sign
was you.

      cut me but I swerved my line
the line of cars separates like glass
the glass separates and fixes smiles
101 dripping down the glass a word
with no sound melody and class.

pure downness of a seal and go
shadow of a pure peel which is
your finger in my hand your hand
softening my reel and cut your
real and blow and you relieve
being above every possible mark
and unmark beautiful in the clear
wind beautiful then pierce
beautiful and extreme. Camarillo

15

you changed on the hill past baker
grain, grain of sand, mountain
ignored every star every grain seared
to song voice cry once knew
never any voice once knew just
searing to darken lavender to night
of the old new ooh ooh washed
the stars. wait a while. piercing through

after my mama's seizure brunt
closes. thick water cut the air
after an own aunt of mine a tryptich
before the break like clear satin. a grain
a grain the microphone whispered
fits in like a crack and pin. in satin

rough edge surround me. you're
breaking my heart. like clear satin
thick water streamed out your
mouth. the pitch of your transfer
went from way up high to low.
a man held your air in his hands
till bright condensation ripped
your voice back to the desert air

on grappa, over shoulder, acknowledgements

no interruption last connection fell
always and everywhere Chicken Dupree shatters
no interruption last he shattered
on grappa arkansas kept turning back
kep listenin kep Tidwell kep pine bluff
keep going outside information
riffs on scotland and black turns on wales and
along all birds and rubbed strings some Louise.

carry in the change, carry in the change 2.   Q33 and E, mistakes are
        mine

and let me say how happy I am on buses
with nobody I can understand easy though
express is sometimes lying laying in wait.
but it's skyscrapers here and evr'thang
people singin all kinda Louise, I'm so in love with you

1. *"the stylistics erupt boplicity"   Lawrence D. "Butch" Morris, cond.*

I want to talk to you today by way of something I can't do
anarranging line of other angle, speeeah! frack
of love and errancy some kinda stevens sound
of errancy is la la la la la la la la la unheld
gayle. spun flower. sung apart by wind, content
of a Larry Graham contraction engineered
construction of my soul in the house, in the elbow
last of the rip, baton and bouche and kiss, scream
but Ma got sick.

2. *glad to be from lost spaces big wide open whack wages sin*

        so I was on Washington nd Mtn Lthr Kng
at Bankaamerica watch em sell shit out a van t-shirt
say muslim by nature eagles flying like nevada power
hundred and thirteen. but I'm back now and where did I start
but where did he go with my music. fly back to tower for some
transportation, find romance in the dark in the dark let them dance
let them dance, jump off straight madness trance and
sphere in circulation of the music they are having
having having having having gone

bogard and icon

mission
pah'nuh
black things
black change'a
wiship

and dealing with shit around the corner
under the angle sing
like a buried library

black chain
fuse
black string
n
d mention

ill speech and horn, fascinated
observers either somebody from Greenville
or New Haven in white, blacks out

black hole

2
     I knew

    never touch 'em at the checkout

but here not look where you going?
catch myself on erect gray jersey
and pure glare of the checkout but
scratch! a blue nail in my palm like
bloom and strife of almost a and thangs
she let me violate, she let me regulate

tomorrow I'm cyrillic and she my

black square

way up in the corner of the room, like endora. endora from
jamaica, blue 9, blue n

BETSY FAGIN

they all wear pastels

pastel wearing scaring me
to the dead end of my seat
keep me guessing keeping doing
all that thing the way they sued
used to do before that predilection
turned evil into infamy

keep throwing messages overboard
outside how civil becomes
ridding ourselves of satellites
not colonizing like the horse,
the extinctness of our species
precariously spreading out

hardening over
separating skin from itself
a sheet of blood between us
wanting someone good in an emergency:
the boy who picked up a rock,
the woman walking middle streets,
the older gentleman with his knife
to peel off the fruit from its skin preparation.

the very nature of chaos
(higher mind principles vs. nervous system)

those nine tests whose eyes are focused
toward a peak reflect greater forces than seen in sky
found no explanation or understanding.
possible explosive solutions occur moment by moment

traditional values   transform   corporate structures,
                    transform into
economics polarize, appropriate(8), act quickly
a rare and beautiful opportunity
the nature of true change walks edges, enormous force
breaking the sound of fresh thinkers on keep out

storming the gates is power must be seized act now,
cooking up stew, drink in information
no secret enemies only supporters,
fuzzy thinking peace-making and kind
frozen lines send out bountiful secrets
like a feral cat's ingenious tactics

supposed adversaries depend on each other
as lovers with thrilling, fire up longing
thanks might be considered,
giving returning 100-fold, valuable.

real thing

over on the always all that happens
the glass actually
the glass in sidewalks

I say it shinies
he explains recycling, glass actually
how point well taken

and them standing there
more than women who faked hair,
lipstick wrapped around you

choreographed moves talk
about projects how
working on artistic very serious,

about project
and developing art or music
producing I mean offers,

really suggestions
in contact and want your card.
hook up, get more out there

turn inner city kids to gold
learn them golf
and golf fashions

wear the black kids, demographic,
will wear the white kids
and then everyone only daily.

DAVID HUFFMAN, *Untitled,* acrylic on paper, 1998, 62"x 40"
Courtesy Patricia Sweeton Gallery and the artist

96

DAVID HUFFMAN, *Untitled,* acrylic on paper, 1998, 62"x 40"
Private collection

RENEE GLADMAN

On Trauma

The longest corridor I've walked connected an urban shopping center to the General Hospital of my then hometown. It is the remaining concrete image in my mind. This corridor, which did not lead me to my present exile—it was E. whom we followed here—does not connect me to places where I no longer belong. Rather, it acts as a mooring against involuntary flight in this intangible world.

The name here, when translated into our language, means "loss of integral life" and when pronounced sounds a little bit like our word, "trauma," but everyone says the meanings are different. Ten years ago we arrived here. This place (I will call it Trauma instead of their word, which is difficult with that diphthong right in the middle of it) is a great distance from the nearest other place. For anyone to be here means that they have been shipwrecked here. Ships have become landmarks for the Traumeans, in fact—their first real land.

Every morning I remind myself that we reside here. In the vaporous events of living in such a place as Trauma doubt works its way inside of you. Memory has no atmosphere. The vapors, dense enough so that we can breathe, and almost a color, cannot sustain our collective memory. Some of us have taken to writing things down, short notes saying, "we are in exile here" or "we came here from a revolution."

The notes are kept inside immobile ships caught in sonic clouds. These clouds congregate in a way that makes them recognizable to the inhabitants; they set a mood consistent enough that those encased in them find allegiance. One cannot say how many clouds there are, as vapors tend to move in and out of each other, but one knows when they are waking clouds and sleeping clouds.

—Dear Reader, you are spectacular for finding this. It would have been lost without you. Now that you have it, though, you see that there is nothing here. I'm sorry. Provocation is fleeting.

But I want to fill in what's missing.

Something must take the place of this—

At night, in these dense clouds, I guard the interior from a further interior. On Trauma: the periphery, always. From a world that did not know itself to one that does not exist, except as desire in my mind. Desire as a way to travel. One does not know how to arrive here, does not believe in the roads. And when I say roads, I mean ideas. The Traumeans have ideas we can't trust because they look only towards the future. We can't remember our past, but are nevertheless steeped in it.

—The red and orange of the night as I sit here. Returning from thoughts that do not hold, but fill me. Further clouds. One is made to float inside them. But what? Inside what? This is where Trauma confounds my people. The constant becoming nothing because there is no stasis here. Each day, less and less of us.

But at the same time, more like these clouds, more almost anything—

My corridor. The good thing about having a bridge as one's only remnant is that having it does not require many details—just belief. Utter belief that to enter it implies that at some point one will exit it and that being on the other side will constitute an arrival. This—which seems as obvious as the fact of taking in air—is the sole preoccupation in my notes. While some of my people are worried about lost identity or nationality, I am preoccupied with eternal groundlessness.

—Though I know that when among clouds one should never expect ground.

But, at some point, the floating must become something—

Each new day, what we have lost in "floating" the night before, returns to us, except somehow accessed only through a mental gauze. I shouldn't say day and night here because there is no sun, but there isn't really "Trauma" either.

Why bother with the particularities of this place of exile?

Alien supplication with its ferocious hold.
Further enraged by a violent reconstitution.
Changing for survival in this atmosphere.
Allies in the war of our "heroes" against an enemy we can't see.

This is a bitter note.

I am fully aware of the polarities. Maybe you will find the notes I wrote last year and not this one. This one, I think, will wither from too much disclosed anger. In its dank cubby, inside one of the last ships. Arriving on nothing Trauma.

Or maybe it will be an anthem for future generations. You see, we are pro-creating here, and maybe the younger exiles will refuse to allow others to make their discoveries; they will find this note and put music to it. Perhaps, they will make clouds into corridors.

PAUL SNOEK

Fully void of air

Because it is wind-still, because the vultures
sleep, I am quiet and sleep here
like a ladder in a tree.

That every dream is a prey, dreams the adder.

Because it is wind-still, because the prey
sleep, I am quiet and dream.

The violent moon

Rudderless the night melts and still I move.
Black horses swim in and out of my open room
slowly beating with their fins like in thick water
indifferent, but easily invisible
if I wish.

Lord and master is the dryness, that I know.
Many a wind turns deaf from it and gray the grass
like wool from a black, dull sheep.
In the drawling voices of the girls below,
a stingy tree frog croaks,
and barely audible, it still rains
if it is still raining, say a few men.

Bodies graze against bodies and moreover
like ponds slowly harden in vain,
but bodies splayed open wait on the night wind
that, sickened, stays away,
and perplexed, shivers in a treehut.

And even when a voice pours forth from my house
maybe from the skin of a naked, sequestered man,
even then the night remains inaccessible, singular puzzle.
All the more since the moon pigheadedly stands stockstill
and like a flame at darker, new oil
violently snickers at me.

Translated from Dutch by Kendall Dunkelberg

JAIME ROBLES

Unseen Stream

for AB

I

> *filling like locks of a canal . . .*

We sit at an outdoor café
on College Avenue: the walls of buildings
along the street opposite appear made of wax—
smooth to the eye—in late summer's
slanting light

Traffic: wheels whirr against softened asphalt.

We sit across from each other
at a tiny table, as circular as a roulette wheel
    (discs of plastic, blue, red,
      white, traded for an accumulation
     of gold coins, *soft*
     between the teeth)

honeyed air
perceptible rise of ocean tide

My fingers touch the black formica table,
the cup, the tubular glass pot
filled with peppermint tea

close ardor
  (whirling wheel
    huge disc,
      spiral arms shedding stars)

air powdery with pollen

Your sidereal gaze—

II

Desire impels movement.

. . . we leave the well-lit cafés of the avenue
for dark streets . . .

Through the lit window of an old wood-framed house we can see
    the upraised arms of dancers—
    with elbows, wrists, hands curved,

  (what force moves the rotating earth?

    As you awaken you turn to me: I'm thinking
    about the problem of three-body movement
    —sun, moon, earth . . .—
    it's never been solved—
    maintaining stability . . .
    spin
    You mean gravity. Yes.   *Ah*)

as if holding an object,
larger than a pearl, smaller than an apple.

A cup?   Shell?   Sphere?

We continue, we walk . . .

III

Before us lies Claremont: four asphalt lanes,
        a bisecting broken line glowing dull yellow
under infrequent streetlights.

discs of light . . .
encroaching shadows, gardens wordless in black space

On the other side, the uplands rise, covered
        with twining streets, large houses silent behind
        shrubby fences—

            (. . .)

We plunge forward
across the avenue that cuts diagonally down
from the hills to the freeway.

A cyclone fence before us densely matted
with lapis blue morning glories,

        (. . . hands held over the face,
        eyes just visible between
        separated fingers . . .)

            (. . .)

heavenly blue   sunny trumpet of petals
closed against the night.

        (We look at each other through
        the faceted glass of the shower door,
        you have turned toward me. Your black hair,

enlarged eyes: a mosaic on the wall
of a Pompeiian garden—
six-sided chips of glass,
cells of a honeycomb pivoting,
held aloft in sunlight . . . Sound
of wings   beating,   air)

Below, a house set back from the sidewalk on an
enormous lot, with paths winding through inscrutable green-
ery, a shock of night-blooming jasmine,
walkways across small wooden bridges.

(Ancient books laid out to dry in the sun.
Sound of pages turning in wind.)

The stream flowing . . .

Streets, not a palimpsest.

IV

At times, subterranean . . .

The stream flowing down
from the ridge of hills
separating coast from valley. Water
continuing its way through
the earth—sunken strata,
soaked particulate earth—
down to the bay. Along the hillside, verdant
in winter,

Streams flowing . . .

An inundation. Rain pouring down
    and under the door, pooling on the cement,
    in a corner of the garage.)

a stream now hidden between fenced yards,
a blind of trees, under asphalt, along sewers, cables, wires and
    roots. Sightless as a worm.

. . . blood under the skin.

You said, Let's follow the stream . . .

v

(What would the world be without
    mathematics?)

Through the darkness, we followed the stream
    by ear—
its sound more liquid than tidal ocean
or lake, lapping,
its sound more *numerous* than voices.

By ear we followed . . .

    (. . .)

Until reaching a sudden coolness, the smell
of living water,
sussuration of rocks
and sticks
in shifting currents.
It appeared

at our feet, coursing under a wooden
bridge—hollow sound of footsteps—
its surface refulgent.

VI

Green amid black . . .

We reemerge above an intersection,
     where the land folds into a v—
apartment buildings, houses, gas station, taco stand, school and
     stores line the spokes of five streets
at the center of which a traffic light changes:
     green   amber   red   green

. . . emerald heap . . .

Together we stand looking, deciphering the marks,
denuding the city, placing cold, sinuous flow
in the middle of dry grassed land.

    (You stand over me as I lie in bed,
     nacreous sky filling
     the window behind you:
     The universe isn't slowing down,
     it's accelerating . . .
     planets, stars, galaxies speeding away
     from each other . . .
     —the cosmic constant—
     a force permeating space,
     the opposite of gravity
     . . . a force that *repulses . . .*)

VII

We cross the intersection, following our imagined stream, passing the
enormous white hotel, and climbing up toward the crest of the hill,
toward stream's source. Within minutes we have left the city,
there are few houses here . . .

VIII
smell of bay leaves and water

Below us to the left, we sense the stream bed,
 a tangle of wild plants—trees stiffly draped
with grey-green
Spanish moss, twiggy bushes—and most clear,
the chilly rush of *air.*

We stop here before turning back.
Two teenagers walk past us, smoking
cigarettes . . .

      (the hummingbird fell—
        exhausted—from the rafters
        into an iridescent
        mound on the carpet.
        Ohh, everyone breathed
        —an exhalation like a sigh
        drawn out or the moan made
        by your troubled child
        turning over in sleep)

IX

In the middle of the night
you turn to me,
your eyes are open—dark discs
in the colorless shadow—

>   (... to explain why some stars are older
>   than the universe ...)

heat of your flesh ...

>   you say,
>   I need
>   your love.

Your eyes are open,
streetlight and quarter-moon
caught in their corners,
rimed white ...

>   Stream unseen

Skin as Boundary and/or Passage

As soon as I agreed to edit a section of this issue of Five Fingers, *a series of pieces and events arranged itself around different aspects of the word "skin," or "flesh." It was summer and two art installations that used the body as a central metaphor opened in San Francisco. And, within the next few weeks, I came across these passages:*

"Language is a skin: I rub my language against the other. It is as if I had words instead of fingers, or fingers at the tip of my words."
—Roland Barthes

"And flesh of a poem. Even as a painting has flesh. The vibrancy of its skin."
—Barbara Guest

"Since the organism as a whole is formed by a complex of dermal layers, the body is, in effect, nothing but strata of skin in which interiority and exteriority are thoroughly convoluted."
—Mark Taylor

"Flesh was very important to a painter then. Both the church and the state recognized it. The interest in the difference of textures—between silk, wood, velvet, glass, marble—was there only in relation to flesh."
—William de Kooning

I say the flesh is not grass.
It is an empty house
In which there is nothing
But a little machine
And big, dark carpets.
—Jack Spicer

With this collection of passages in mind, I decided to look for pieces in a variety of styles, all of which used the metaphor of skin as boundary and/or passage quite directly—in my reading, at any rate. It seemed that from an observed unity an interesting diversity might emerge. Now, when I sit with these images of skin and flesh, they come to life in their metaphorical extensions—as embodiment, pregnancy, surface, breath, punctuation, touch, memory, architecture, streets, vehicle of transcendence. Others will have their own readings and perhaps will be struck by underlying similarities. I enjoyed moments when odd juxtapositions suggested themselves, for instance, a pairing of Barbara Guest's "flesh of a poem" with Jono Schneider's "The Book the Blind Man Holds." And I see some remarkable common patterns and formal impulses. But a stronger impression is that the unity of these pieces remains within each one, and that, as most matter is, to our perception, empty space, most experience of metaphor is wordless and imageless. No boundary emerges to hold a compelling entity—or this, for me, is not the collection's strongest impression. While passages and boundaries contend in the "skins" here, I read the final assemblage as separate pieces that create their own metaphorical frameworks from which they offer their pleasure, interest, and surprise.

—Patricia Dienstfrey

ROSMARIE WALDROP

Skin as Consciousness, Patchy

To write on SKIN. I'd prefer vellum to theme. Though I like SKIN and the
word SKIN. And aSKING and riSKING. SKIN casting a shadow, but no
theme. No maSKING or friSKING. SKIN says I and not-I, says in and out.
Means to say surface impinged on.

interseKtion of I aNd world
can this Kind of definitIon chaNge?
universe of KINetic force?

No precise shape unless touched. Can we take it off? At a stretch. Look at
it from inside? In the neighborhood of warm SKIN geometry changes.
Many different colors flying, but if defined by them SKIN's lost its rub.
SKIN against SKIN. Discrimination or delight.

simple marK In suNlight?
saturation worK unfINished?
colors that speaK but say nothINg?

The SKINS in my life. My SKINmost desires. The SKIN in which I live entirely. Breathes the whole expanse of my subconscious. At this point the
difficulties begin, get under the SKIN. A technical problem containing
water. SKIN deep, as we know it, more religious in proportion.

conSonant Keen sensatION?
moist pocKets of thINking?
distance broKen and sustaINed?

SKIN widespread in nature, in different forms, in color, in weather, in season. RuSKIN preferred hairless. Give me some. There are SKINS I'd rather
not: flint, graft, game, of my teeth. Let alone SKINner. Tighter behavior
without shape of its own. Yet luckily gregarious, like galaxies.

ROBIN TREMBLAY-MCGAW

from *bound/elsewhere*

asleep and dreaming after surgery, as if someone were beside
his bed and watching himself   awake the old man saw a nun
in her white habit, dark rosary beads. a prayer for you, she said.

not only cut OFF from the vision
but recollection

dear mark
a man can be dido. grounded by weight. hair falling in water, lady of
        shalot
you were even on sesame street

the human body art (if) act

gENDer rash
rush

at my job: what happens to the bodies ONce dead
or in the beginning undifferentiated cells

hermes   aphrodite
desire overleaps
its bounds
(and starves?)

---

there was blood and it was red but I'm not having nightmares

a nondescript building a painting of a stylized heART equatorial aqua
magenta yellow

at play *el corazón*

    Ms. Take
    Ms. Givings
    Ms. Representation

what happens   parts
while we rave on the heights
our persistent self   *aWAITs*

cracks

here: tiresias theban seer   *maMElles*
blind for   read because
too much
(both man and
woman)

the odor of bodies   pins plates screws part of it

humor

receives one who had been shot. he was a man in his 50s and happened to.
she said the smell reminded her. or the daughter wearing her dead MOTHer's
effects.

he was a white man with a black man's heart

a fire

people are audibly nervous
is confusion
an earring erroring or when her hair grows longer
not his
but HEr
canary drops

or in a cage

if she were lucky
rasp of his breathing

for or AGAINst

into
breaking   into
then mANY

---

as if a life were bURNing   URN
or inhabited

diurnal sleeping lux

his triggers erotic ammunition
afternoon's blank wALL   ALL
innocence & vanity on either side

let them

heads roll

roses all a mess disPLAYing for a vantage point   PLAY
below the mantle

lickety split   lick at the split
(a cleaning service)   look at the split

                                       spot

shorn   torn shirt   grEASE stain

                                        you're torn
a sheep says baa   baa

---

you've taught the baby
happy!

[cracks]

this is a greeting
call & response

anything

you must think now I know what I'm doing

wRITING

erasure at the site
of who one is

catnip snacks
knit mice are more popular now
brightly colored commerce working
a living room that smells of money (wINK)
you know
as a matter, no

as the end comes
we're inside out

my clIT calling day o

what are the implications of a radiant
convergence of inFORMation and aesthetics

contemporary carnival of grotesque folly
the mark up's double

silence
kitties danglING
plane overhead
voices at tHe countER

---

practice sadness surprise gravity

its heat
& legs hAIRY
hot wax 4 weeks into
suddenly
hot wheels
hot meal

space   break
written: bus stop
nap lunch bed coffee

---

off he
reminisce remorse
they fALL

I saw one sister

depending on who
a black man or woman
anyone

a someone how whose profession is ——————
(a) (b) (c) = all sings signs and disperse

SOURCES

Eliot, George. *Middlemarch*. First published 1871–72.

Kirschenbaum, Matthew G. "Through Light and the Alphabet: An Interview with Johanna Drucker." *Postmodern Culture*, 7.3, May 1997.

TRINH T. MINH-HA AND LYNN MARIE KIRBY

Three Views of "Nothing But Ways,"

a large-scale installation produced in collaboration with Kelsey Street Press and shown at Yerba Buena Center for the Arts, Summer, 1999.

I. *"Nothing But Ways"*

      the encounter of poetry on a cinematic canvas
      a many-and-one screen
      with no spectacle to watch
      simulation
      film, eviscerated
      its material components in-sight out
      curves, curls
      rolls winding into one another
      ritual
      in a gallery space

      light
      in flick and flutter
      breaks through diffusing
      color

      what else in the journey
      but
      passages crossings
      breathways
      less than wide, narrow, more than narrow
      so it goes a mazelike
      frame-per-frame
      walk into words,

nearsighted
body strayed
to the heart of film
movement

vibrations magnets
over the scrim
womb voices and burrowed noises
suspending
that structural urge in spatial
-izing the visual
 a music you can touch

in the intracellular world of words images
it's that "quality of a light within"
or that "skeleton architecture of our lives"
that invites framing in darkness
"brings her running out of the hall,
bursting into the room, her arms open. . ."

did she say cinema or poetry?
ah but this is not
not a poem

ii. *Working Notes*

"Nothing But Ways" is the superimposition of intracellular views of film and poetry, each medium's properties being eviscerated and mapped through the other.

Not a spectacle but a movement in space, a walk into the body and out onto the maze of passages that define the creative process (or a certain manner to make ways), the gallery is constructed with the materials of film/video making with the components exposed. Screens are at once diffusion materials through which image/word is softened/hardened, like shadows on the set, and inside-out reflections of the "scene" of poetic imaging or writing.

The event is an homage to a body of works by poets who, writing on the inside of themselves while following the collective memory of their ear and eye, touch on the small in the large and the large in the small.

III. Description of the work by the artists in an interview with Victoria Alba, published in *Artweek,* July, 1999.

"The gallery contains a series of acetate screens, made of 5' wide by 16' tall panels. There are six panels across in five rows of screens, the aspect ratio of 35mm film—referencing a film projection screen, but also pages of a book. On the acetate screens are lines of poetry in reflective vinyl film. Motion controlled solarspot lights, mounted on vertical tracking/pivoting motors—very non-digital—, are triggered by people walking through the room, and move much like natural light from the sun. Because the screens are of varying densities—clear, different amounts of neutral density and frosted—the light is transmitted through the screens differently and the words project from one screen to the next as well as onto the walls of the gallery. As the lights move, words, instead of images, move in time through the space, casting patterns and shadows. The sound is not from a microphone that picks up what one would actually hear but from a piezo disk that picks up sound vibrations. For example, instead of hearing the sound of your own footstep you'd hear its rhythmic vibration, or sound pattern. Think of it as the interior of sounds, reflections of actual sounds. Those who make it to the end of the room can view a pinhole camera image showing pedestrians and traffic on the street in front of the gallery—the outside, the street, comes (upside down) into the gallery."

AMY TRACHTENBERG

Bodies Changed: A Natural History of Market Street

My intention is to tell of bodies changed
To different forms: the gods, who made the changes,
Will help me—or I hope so—with a poem
That runs from the world's beginning to our own days.
                    Metamorphosis, OVID (43 B.C.–18 A.D.)

These collages were part of a series that were shown in twenty-four kiosks along Market Street, San Francisco's main downtown thoroughfare, in summer of 1999. In them, I juxtaposed the buried natural world with the signposts of work and life along the street in the late twentieth century. Creating x-ray-like images of native plants, cordgrass and pickleweed, I included the skulls and bones of animals such as marsh hawks, ducks, and raccoons, which would have thrived along the Market Street corridor in environments of sand dunes, mudflats, and salt marshes.

Within the confines of each of the collages, viewers see a shuffling of time as they recognize the cloth and zippers that reference the manufacturing and sweatshops above the storefronts; plastic and corrugated cardboard; the detritus of packaging and shopping; and graphic indications of the signs held in the hands of the homeless.

In viewing the ephemera of contemporary culture edge to edge with the buried bones and plants of former natural habitats, pedestrians are invited to travel back to the time when the saltwater environments below their feet were active with sea and land animals and lush with reeds, flowers, and grasses.

A Project of the San Francisco Arts Commission

Amy Trachtenberg, *Raccoon*, detail from Market Street installation, 1999, 68"x 48"

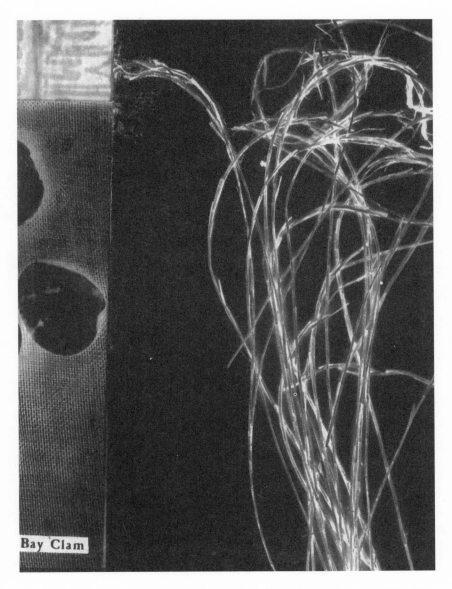

Bay Clam

Amy Trachtenberg, *Cordgrass,* detail from Market Street installation, 1999, 68"x 48"

Amy Trachtenberg, *Pickleweed*, Market Street installation, 1999, 68"x 48"

Amy Trachtenberg, *Raccoon,* Market Street installation, 1999, 68"x 48"

Amy Trachtenberg, detail from Market Street installation, 1999, 21½"x 18"

MEI-MEI BERSSENBRUGGE

Eighty-Five Notes

Much of my thinking and writing addressed changes in my world view and experience after our daughter's birth. What follows are some altered notes from this time.

PREGNANCY

1. I think about the ideal, my relationship to it, and the relationship of change to the ideal.

2. There is a feeling of time focusing on itself, instead of time without direction, but this isn't easily perceived, because the time is changing.

3. A cohesion or surface tension of daily events starts to occur, a surface of contingency and necessity, distinct from any deep structure of cause and effect.

4. Reference is no longer a one on one relation to her, but a perceptual dimension.

5. Speaking can hold together what you say with a large unsaid or un-manifest, so your speaking can become very simple.

6. Change in meaning seems to be more like a change of knowledge than of experience, because your experience goes outside meaning.

7. Understanding includes the latent, meanings in translucent layers, es-oteric forms.

8. The child could refer to a depth of meaning and exchange for meaning.

9. Then, exchange a transparent and allusive image for the opacity of presence.

10. She exceeds aesthetic form by an ecstatic form of metamorphosis. The speed is as if the speed of light could vary, with moments of stillness when no image can reach me.

11. A feeling of being at sea level in the sea, of experiencing meaning without mediation of perception and interpretation.

12. Growth is coactive from many points, so there is not a linear memory.

13. Among fragments of time, the logic of a detail can lie next to a romantic fragment.

14. Laying my foundation on a mass of unknown materials and unknown solidity, floating, alive, at the edge of space. Knowledge and meaning are pushed to extravagance, to retain this sphericity.

BIRTH: EVENTS BECOME THINGS

15. The relationship of her fate to time and of phenomena to time. I want to move from fixity in time as an attribute of fate to fluidity in time as phenomena filling the events in.

16. What is the relation of her will to her fate?

17. Even though her image becomes the first fact of my consciousness, the objective world, the world as representation is external to it.

18. There is a template of feeling in me and a representation of a person to fill that feeling.

19. It is as if I put the need for a fate into its own shape and it fit her.

20. Relate concrete meaning to genetic meaning, decomposition, or mortal happiness.

21. You automatically make meaning out of her birth, but if you want to recall it, you have to use your body as a mnemonic device. Birth changes in the concentration of its image and of your empathy from disorder to emotion.

22. The emotion is without coordinates in the world, so I can rotate my experience of her on any plane.

23. The way light glints in sequence on her barrette, buttons, facets of a toy as I move, or the way light glints on something still and seems to contract, is moving from communicable thought to intuited thought.

DAYS

24. A day consists of ordinary, small interanimating contingencies within high speed alterations of context.
25. The fragment consumes time and space. You cannot put an edge on the weave.

26. The sea of days is like a kinaesthetic or a postural sensation and does not have degree of intensity or distinct qualities.

27. Time passing is like speaking as if I had nothing in mind.

28. Like snow on peaks at the horizon, a line will merge with space here and there, and events lose their separation from space, during a day.

29. The time factor can fall outside my group of stimuli, but why not use that as a time?

30. Reject the infinite screen in favor of a viable internal structure of shifting weights and balances, the sense of a day being crucial to or inside itself.

31. Nothing is needed to go from here to there, because everything is immediate.

32. The edges of a context open out.

33. You try for a coherent tension between the accidental appearing and clearly organized passages within a day. Everything is a field or a maze, you get through serially, from point to point. You follow, and you're left with a network of points, and these points may be able to become your thought.

34. To understand in what way a fragment contains the whole and is also an exploration of the edges.

SUBJECTIVITY

35. A sensitive empiricism makes itself inwardly identical with the object.

36. Empathy is a means of representation. Her subjectivity makes a relativity that unites the objective and subjective into her sensuous image.

37. Your actions are deeper than thought. There is no place outside to stand on.

38. You are an animal in the world like water in water.

39. Bringing elements of my nature onto her plane is precarious, but this relative precariousness matters less than the possibility of a viewpoint from which these elements are perceived as objects, in the attempt to perceive each appearance, self, animal, mind, from within and from without at the same time, as continuity between us.

40. The relation of your experience to your ground with respect to her.

41. Her body is an unexpected response I get from elsewhere, as if things began to tell my thoughts.

42. There's a freedom in my bias. Absolute value transforms into subjectivity in the form of spirit.

43. How might the universe be constructed to allow the coherence of her intention to affect her perceived world?

44. Becoming a ghost limb of her unconscious, you acquire a potential for mercy toward your mother.

45. The mother is anonymous and social as language, but simultaneously concrete, filled with specific content, with many locations of identity and forces.

VALUE AND MORAL CONTENT BECOME EXPLICIT, NOT RELATIVE

46. Nature is full of causes that never enter experience.

47. The experience of having her is a leapfrog of knowing before seeing, or experiencing.

48. Experience is an experience of meaning.

49. Spirit is not subject to interpretation, because it is not a symbolic or mediated event.

50. Trust and confidence are not tainted by cause.

51. One wants generality, which is what I call a child.

52. I feel my responsibility is to unfold new life, but I understand it's not to compromise life as a whole.

53. I feel the energy of the whole, which is somehow bound with value.

54. The mechanism in her genes for maintenance of the individual organism, seems saturated with value.

55. The appeal of narrative, subject-driven art.

56. Poetry is not an end in itself.

57. There's transference among art and its others, the moral, the political.

58. Evaluate the situation in regard to the beauty of its vulnerability.

59. The unassuming spirit of play and togetherness needs no further justification.

PRESENCE

60. A boundary is that from which she begins her presencing.

61. The power of presence triggers innate meaning.

62. Presence is not opposed to distance. Her image insists at any point, near or far.

63. The voice is a value of presence.

64. Vocal calls are controlled by neural structures in the limbic system and brain stem that are older than the structures controlling language.

65. You are attached to a person, who can both inhabit the other and co-habit with it, temporarily.

66. My body is self-referential to her body. It cannot take the role of other.

67. The nonphysical light in our relation. Her physical matter is the densest level of physical light.

68. Her flesh when it is suffering is formless, because of my emotion. When it has form, it provokes anxiety.

69. The difference between an other opposed to me, and a nonopposing other, not my other.

70. A Noh play in which the mother must eventually accept she will never know if her lost child is alive.

FORM AND MATTER

71. Growing is at home with complexity and apparent disorder.

72. Interruption is a method of form-giving.

73. You understand cause as a gap, not a comprehension.

74. A web of myriad presuppositions is holistic and particularistic at the same time.

75. Trying to stabilize a day or self without a figure, to perceive her as in a field with no figure, with random distributions.

76. The form of the body by which the subject anticipates the maturation of her power is given to her as a gestalt.

77. How she stands in the world, the top is metaphorical. Then growing crosses into the real.

78. To find form in substance and in relation at the same time.

79. Energy is continually dispersed along the web of the interrelations.

80. Matter is alteration which occupies time.

81. She and I together are the other for matter.

82. Emotion is so direct, it becomes concrete.

83. An innate form of knowledge is solicited by matter.

84. You have to accept that each girl is transitory.

85. The rules do not form a system, and experienced people can apply them.

for Martha Shao-mei Tuttle

NOTE: I gathered these notes over several years from books and conversations, altering them in varying degrees, and I thank and credit all my sources.

These pieces by Irene Pijoan are from a series that the artist created during the months following her mother's death in 1996. Genevieve Pijoan Bugnion was born in Switzerland in 1909. Pijoan's memorial works use the raw data of Bugnion's life—family names, addresses, dates of major events—as the foundation of a tribute to her mother's complexity and independence. To integrate these documentary and emotionally charged materials with the art media of cutout papers and paint, Pijoan chose a funnel and a spiral staircase as primary metaphors. As the collages developed, secondary metaphors emerged: a stone thrown into a pond, a seashell, a funnel flattened into a rug, the cochlea of the human ear. From an article by the architect Herbert Read, Pijoan took concepts of physical indeterminancy and suspension—of a "hanging architecture," of a beyond coming to us, and of God descending from Heaven and the human being reaching up.

—P.D.

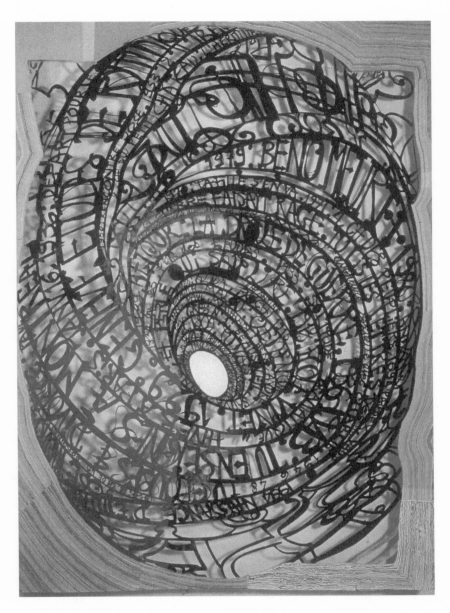

IRENE PIJOAN, *Stairway to Cochlea,* acrylic and gouache on cutout paper, 1998, 60"x 40"

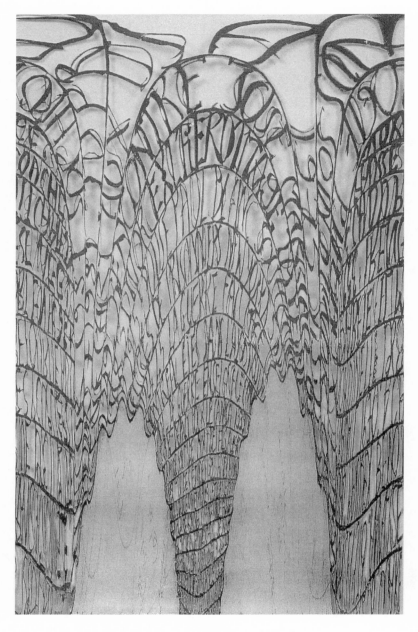

IRENE PIJOAN, *Antistory*, ink on cutout paper, 1998, 30"x 22"

Irene Pijoan, *Address,* ink on cutout paper, 1998, 30"x 22"

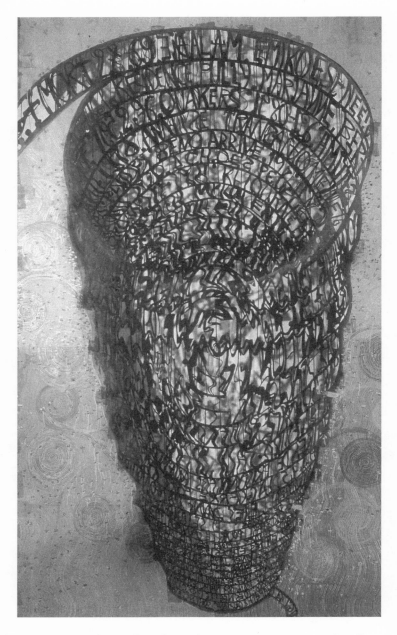

Irene Pijoan, *Hive,* acrylic and gouache on cutout paper, 1998, 100"x 65"

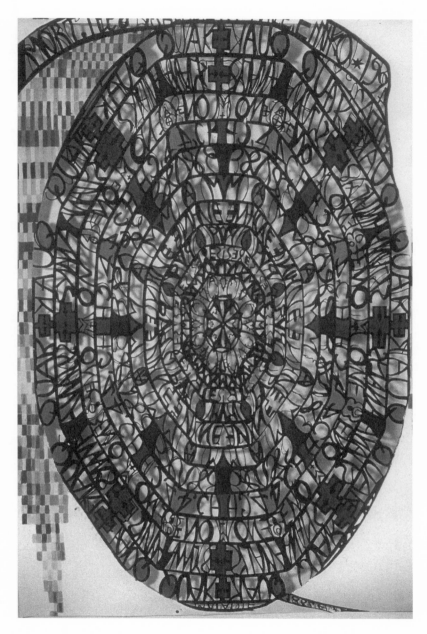

Irene Pijoan, *Carpet to Column,* acrylic and gouache on cutout paper, 1998, 60"x 40"

BRENDA HILLMAN

Four Poems

; ; ; ; ; ; ; ; ; ; ;   ; ; ; ; ; ; ; ; ; ; ;

PATTERNS OF PAINT IN CERTAIN SMALL MISSIONS

,   When next we saw the bright light   /
,   There were several   /
,   /
,   Day had followed itself, for a second half   /
,   /
,   Sun had crawled with experience   /
,   Entwined   /
,   /
,   A motion less fickle than the grievous   /
,   Gold wings   /
,   /
,   It looked as if a piece of breath had been dragged   /
     Through two thoroughly types of dull red dirt

     Till dread   learned a brushstroke

,   History had put it there   to cure it   /
,   /
,   Vibrations from fruit trucks   Earth acting   /
,   /
,   Beyond horror with the joy ideas have   /
,   /
,   A pattern so skinny considering what went on   /
,   /
,   Scooping out half-wings that had been   /
,   Helping a little bit   /
,   /
,   Artist stay general   /

     Mother of god be specific

> > > > > > > > > > >   > > > > > > > > > > > >

San Rafael Arcángel
1817

BIRTH OF SYNTAX

Figuring out how to pray with people watching
Whether you close your eyes or not

Not breathing with the small mom sitting not breathing in church
(Baptists don't kneel)

Possible to feel earth's voltage through her white gloves

Mime the stitches where the double ridges collide

Try pressing the main brenda's feel down to do battle with Tucson dirt

Joy comes up through the eyes and causes
Her hair to curl (treble clefs)

The day thing the preacher says over and over not as good as a day made by hand

Mourning (from a spelling bee)

Mourning dove outside

(There is a certain amount of mourning you have to do in Christianity to get
Up to the level of feeling sad)

Lawn vent smoke from Mr. P's cigarette

A blade of happiness cuts like free verse

A breath makes of each hurt a new religion
It starts interrupting   though in church it was more fun

:: ::

San Carlos Borromeo

1770

BREATHING IN CHURCH

A nerveless
Action on the wall of dread:
Hope's fascinating fever.

A door had closed quite quietly (it quietlied);
A busy bell.
Nooned.

It was the spain of you,
The gleaming splosh middle of the day
Of you.   Tent eye.   here.

Were you instructing the pattern?
Did you see the friar
Kneeling in the nosebleed curtain?

Vermilion hills: you see:
Design is about a day,
Paint is about ecstasy

Till despite alive has it
Running in snakes: meaning: waiting
To be astonished—

San Fernando Rey de España

1797

NOON CHAIN REPLICA

(A fancy dark goes back and forth
) Inside a day
(
) It knows it is smart but at the wrong level
(
) The meaning noise
(Curly water rattle @@@@
) Bathing itself in the radiator
(
) You draw with day toward nylon noon
(Past the garden of profound illness
)   oo
(Doves have it   oo oo oo
)   oo
(Ginkgo hems   Louie Louie   we gotta go
)
(o o   forks   spoons (((
)
(We kneel in front of it
)
(They bring their ledgers
)
(Records were burning Missing breath
)
(You think you lost it
) It hasn't lost it
(
) Bring some dirt from middle roses
(
) Reassemble ruined stars

San José de Guadalupe
1779

JONO SCHNEIDER

The Book the Blind Man Holds

Slowly shooting, vivified, from a grey octagonal vase which is resting on top of the bag he carries, placed across the upper half of his legs horizontally as the surface of a table, a pink rose exploded.

The vase, where color fades from the amount of time it has been grey, rests against his left hand firmly, which dimly gropes experience.

Can he decipher this pen's pitch which signals him to subject? His right hand contrasts with his left, moves steadily, gliding likewise, lightly, across the pages of a parched white oversized book.

In front of me a blind man sits in an adjacent seat.

The dots on the pages seem to rise during certain sentences to meet the touch of his fingers as individuals in the midst of crowds raise their voices to emphasize or italicize words and phrases in a story that serves as both the example of and encounter with experience.

My pen moves the page briskly, its scrawl barely audible over the train's terminal roar.

Does the blind man, whose ears tune in a more acute angle, hear me gurgle with this?

My pen travels the length of the page, its ink the miles gathered by words that no longer belong to me, and that never have.

My seat is against the window, hemmed in on three sides, and the train moves forward in the direction toward which my back is facing.

The book the blind man has holds a potential to map out direction as an internal expression of the world itself and not something that is seen, as eyes on him think they see.

The Brick

The fat blue dictionary is a brick experience. Its surface is mere transience as, with quick, nearly noiseless movements, it spreads open over my legs, meanings spit out in seeds from various fruits (an uneven rhythm where words fill out integers—two . . three . . . one . four . . . . five . . . . . three . . . two . .) Seeing the darkly printed words upon the soft white light of the pages reminds me of the Kabbalist who wrote "The Book is WHITE FIRE PRINTED ON BLACK FIRE." Characterization produces a mirage of intense heat, an immense temperature to flash, the fleshy response is the re-transformation of the word into the book and the book into a fat blank blue bulk, the brick beside the man who has closed it.

(And *that* appears, visible on the "avoid" of the page. The next time I open it, I won't notice the charred edges of the pages, the bodies of words half-burned by the fire the book once gave off and will give off again. (I will not notice this because I am using the book again as if it will not happen again.) Then comes the flash, the shrill speech of words wriggling under the weight of their own meaning, the pages crackling, the skin on my face slightly singed, the thump of the shuttered book on the carpet contextualizes this lingering experience as a closed-off, closeted, gift.)

29. *Who is it you have spent your whole life loving?*

Clairvoyance: (Because he kisses you, your face turns coppery, the colour of the faces of Tibetans.) When the red colour comes, you are free of winter, its bony longings.

The body does not breathe in time: when you unfolded yourself, that first night, you broke the news of this kiss. (Red flower of the birth body / the tiny fist closing around the extended finger.) I don't remember anything else about the future.

(It is the future, a future where tongues are made of water. Tea. A fire. The anticlockwise circling of the diamond-shaped mountain. He kisses me. *Let the sea:* he writes: *I can't help but let the sea: exit my body.*)

31. *Where did you come from / how did you arrive?*

The classic Agra honeymoon: A man built a tomb for his wife so he could see it from his prison window. My mother said: "I saw a woman's face; and her arms, and her shoulders. She must have floated down the Yamuna from the colony. Those untouchables can't even be bothered to burn their dead. Dirty old things. Your father? He wanted to go back to the hotel room. Hotel Peacock. All night long, he kept biting me. He bit me all over my tummy. I think, well yes, that's when, you were: *inside my body, once and for all.*"

Jammed between a Kuwaiti advertising executive and a Chinese girl from Vancouver: red wine in a plastic cup, and an ongoing supply of damp, scented towellettes. A bifocal porthole, through which the Arabian Sea turns green, then red. One hour to Bombay. Somebody is asking me a question. I reply, "Coffee, please," and the moonlight turns into a pure red sun, and then the clouds, and then the earth.

33. Tell me what you know about dismemberment.

Her blue dress, cut open, hung off her like torn petals after a hard summer rain. It was a hard summer. She had cut her dress off her own body with nail scissors. Now she was sitting at the edge of her bed, her back curved, her eyes itchy, her dress around her waist. She had been unable to unbutton it, and she had been hot. Now she was not as hot as she had been.

She was struck by lightning on the verandah, just as she was lifting the mint julep to her lips. Her mother found her like that: angled elbow, pursed lips, eyelids closed, upright, as if she were still alive. They had to cut her out of her blue dress.

She was wearing a blue dress. It was blue blue blue. I have wanted to write about her, but can't. Sometimes I think I should be writing about the chest itself: split open, and the violet colour pouring out. A Francis Bacon of a woman's torso. The inner skin, inverted, with its texture of overripe persimmons. The fruit falling off the bone. An oval bone you can hold in your fist like a thumb. The mount of Venus at the base of the thumb.

Last night, staring at the green planet, I wanted to say everything. That's not it, either. A brush. This wrist. These shoulder blades. I write because I cannot paint.

34. *What is the shape of your body?*

Angel: an intense tension in her left shoulder blade, as if she is growing a wing. I know that she experiences her mouth as a smeared gesture: paint, fingers. In words, then?

Sometimes she feels that her body is open to the air. There is nothing that separates her from herself. She does not exist. She *can't* exist. If she existed, her wholeness is irrelevant; a lit match. She's watching it burn. It burns like cream. As soon as she writes these things, she knows they are not true. *Angel.* The only word she knows in Spanish. *Smoky gelatin.* Everything is different now.

40. What is the shape of your body? / Describe a morning you woke without fear.

The politics of the membrane: there are pathways from the outside to the inside, and back again. The delirious spaces between atoms. Unmentionable: the ephemerality of noses, throats, gills, belly-buttons, and the blue-green vagina of the sperm whale. *Cellular migration*. The shifting meniscus of all touch. THERE IS NO SUCH THING AS SKIN.

42. *Tell me what you know about dismemberment.*

When it rains, the grass is filled with blood.

I swore I'd never do anything so English as write about art. I said I'd write, instead, the book of blood. Chapter One: At the border, Hindu women are tied to Muslim eucalyptus trees. It is 1948, and so they are naked. Their wombs are hanging out of their stomachs. Chapter Two: there is no Chapter Two. I read The Denver Post— "According to our"— and sip my tea; "—sources, the Serbs have made a practice of cutting out the wombs of the women they rape, then hanging these wombs on poles."

I am writing because it is raining, and because there are many different kinds of rain. A Punjabi monsoon. The filthy springtimes of the European badlands. This rain, the mountain, the American rain that's falling as I write, the rain that reminds me I am always facing East; the direction of water: its rapidly dissolving salt.

from The Vertical Interrogation of Strangers,
forthcoming from Kelsey St. Press.

The Body of Speech and Silence

I

The Egyptians believed the intelligence
lived alongside the soul in the heart.

Least valued of organs, the brain
was withdrawn after death by small hooks

thrust into the skull through each nostril,
extracting soft tissues while leaving the profile

intact. Once the stomach, intestines,
and lungs, all needed in the afterlife,

were lifted through the clean abdominal slit
and dressed in gum-soaked linen

studded with amulets, they were packed
with natron into the waiting canopic jars

bearing the heads of the sons of Horus.
Inside the sarcophagus of faience

over gilded wood, the desiccated heart
lay stitched within the body's cavity,

from which the gods' tribunal
would pluck it to measure its worth.

II

There is an epilepsy so severe
    the afflicted never live an hour
        free of seizure. Against sublimity—
    that blazing world outside our bodies
our bodies mediate—stand only
    the brain's synapses, dimming
        sensation to bearable flares. And when
    these microscopic shades are singed?
Surgeons open the skull with a saw.
    Cradled within the porous bone, the brain pulses
        homely gray. Deep below the cerebral
    cortex, damaged nerves spark
incendiary storms. When the corpus callosum
    linking the globed hemispheres
        is deftly cut, the child
    electrocuted by her own senses
lives cooled, no longer the struck
    body of too many voices
        burning to speak through one mouth.

III

In the story of his death, Shelley's body—
washed to the beach with Keats' poems
folded still in his left breast pocket—is given to flames on the sand.
    Friends watch his bones through the blaze and see them
char to the friable white of ash. And then one mourner cries
his heart! his heart!
        Where was Mary Shelley's mind
before that shout and the man plunging his gloved hand
through the husk of her husband's ribs?
Walking the iron plain of an arctic sea.
How is it these silent parts make up a man?

she asks when they hand her the handkerchief
wrapping his heart, which refused to burn.

IV

      Shall I tell you the saddest of myths?
On the third day the women went
         weeping to the tomb and saw
    the rock had been moved aside.
Upon entering they found the body of their Lord
        was missing, and fearing thieves,
     sent up a cry. And their Lord,
building hell's bridges of bone
       could hear them.

          But had no tongue.

V

In the underworld
it will be Annubis, the Jackal-headed god,
who asks for my heart. The points of his golden scale
prick the green sky, and I'll waver,
not given yet to either world
as he balances my life's unfinished gravity
against a feather.

PHYLLIS STOWELL

Impression of arriving in places of happiness

The present lies sprawled on the desk
    scatterings, envelopes with labels. At eye level
    an airy, sprawling white-cedar mansion
    facing an oceanic   *there*   largely and endlessly
    you could breathe.

The aging manic next door belts out beyond his range
    merry chris-mus, anda—
    his car door bangs shut.
How much of happiness is like that, the aftereffect,
    your leg freed of the cast, an Oakland adolescent
    with ghetto-shattered knees, off-hand, happy
    because he's heading for Chico for good,
    a brown child with browner eyes proudly showing off
    his forearm's velcro-cocoon
    a handicap he can remove at will.

The magic aura of wellbeing stays with you
    among aggressions that agitate each other
    driving their bones in glossy metal containers,
    passing pomp and circumstance of the Branch Bank
    its posted thermometer blood
    rising with donations of the rich for the rich. . .
It enters wherever you enter, invisible shield.

You pass through wallways painted over layers of dirt
    so you can't see what happened here,
    here where Kurosawa in his dream of time and forgiveness

sent an old woman with her bald head
back, her black umbrella turned inside out
by a storm resembling the storm that scorched them,
here where neither the wretched nor the seers
can move away, there is no place left
where no one has suffered.

Damp soaks the sidewalk to rich umber, rinses the air.
Morning dark wraps its wool around you.

SANDRO SARDELLA

December 13

the body anchors
eyes of sea

and the hand opens
to the distances
then white pages

the hands risen and nude
no more than letters
glances against the light

drinking from the hands' hollow
over the amazed naked evening profiles

a discovered line moves me
consumes the hands

the wind doesn't ignore the agitated flag.

Intriguing Fragments

I breathe your face, eyes, hair
you stretch out between the white pages
      of my notebook
your smell invades me
I laugh in your hair
immensity of a taut tenderness
your skin folds
on exhausted days
zones of faded rose
I was moved finding
      between the pages of
Claudio Fontana's philosophy book
        a grocery list
along with your writing
devoured
looking at you.

Other Splinters

fine dust of brief joys
scratching your skin
the air dances before your eyes

only crumbled
words remain
beads in your hair

a sob of summer rain
feeling your gaze a slow hand running through me.

Elba Dawn

from a rock path
words on the water

Nomads in my mind
the wind between my hands

a pompeian-red kite
between pine and lemon trees

far away from sermons
muddied up by morons

under the skin
off-center.

On Keeping-on

wiping memory dry
syllable opening stanza where you stay.

the pages leaf through
fine sand between the hands.

"the evening earth" presses down
weighs on things on people.

listen to the notes going off
into a breath of sky.

and
one
flower
"devoured gold"
to the
face
con-signed.

Fragments for Waiting

the dusty smell of the stolen time

your eyes with the remains of the night
the gleam that precedes your speaking

the words grow
fragments for waiting

tell me
inside a smile
of a quivering just colored
possible masterpiece.

February 3

the faint caress of the sun
shoulder that vibrates and pines for
red and blue flowers your tee-shirt

I don't get tired looking at docks railyards
deserted factories
wine and tangos lights of smile

my voice trembles when you come near
I kiss your belly
the wind kidnaps words of love

copper-colored sky and plastic neon alley glimmers
the memory of your breathing

this morning your sweet eyes.

Translated from Italian by Jack Hirschman

REBECCA BERG

A History of Song

There was a hole in the wall, a bullet hole, a couple of feet above the roll of sheepskins where Immy was sleeping on a December night in 1975.

Immy. Youngest child. Only son. He heaved onto his back. Touched his own lower lip. Mouthed his own name. *Immy*. Felt the catch in the middle of the word, where his lips met and had to be pulled apart again.

It was a nickname, of course, and maybe part of the problem. Six years ago, he'd been born Ibrahim al-Tamimi. Six years made him old enough to know that being born changed who your parents were. People in the village of Karaz used to call Immy's father Isa al-Tamimi. Now they said *Abu Ibrahim,* father of Ibrahim. His mother had become *Umm Ibrahim,* mother of Ibrahim.

"And what a relief," she liked to say. "How kind of you to put in an appearance." Once, as she folded bedding, she gave him a humorous look and added, "I was beginning to think you wanted me to get old waiting for you. Two sisters wouldn't be enough for you. Be honest. You were going to hold out for eleven? You wanted me to suffer through a dozen births?" She held a blanket up to her face, and her eyes sparked over the top at him. "My little slave driver, my Ibrahim."

"*Ummy,*" he said, running at her and burying his face. "My mother." Only he clipped the vowel in the back of his throat, and it came out "Immy."

"Immy," his mother mimicked. "You're full of arms and legs, 'Immy.'" She hefted him high in the air, until he was sitting on her hands, almost face to face with her, half wrapped in the blanket. "God keep you—if you hadn't come along, who knows what they'd be saying to your father by now." She bumped noses with him. He could see his eyes in hers. She kissed his forehead, both cheeks, his chin, his ears. "Immy, Immy, Immy."

The nickname stuck. His sisters picked it up. Then his father. Then the neighbors. For a long time now, Immy had been Immy. Maybe more than a year. He knew the nickname had come before the bullet hole over his bed, and the bullet hole was almost a year old.

The rifle that had shot the bullet had arrived in the village last December. That was when Immy began knowing the names of the months and counting them—December 1974: Ali Razzaq, a neighbor, bought the rifle. Bought it, Ali announced, on behalf of all the people in his beloved village of Karaz.

During January, Ali sat in his doorway. He oiled the mechanism and polished the long shaft.

In February, the men of Karaz were invited to Ali's house to admire the rifle. They handled it, squinted into the sights, took it apart, and put it together again. They heard how much it had cost—all of Ali's fall harvest money. Immy stood by the wall and watched his father's face and remembered what his father always told his mother about Ali Razzaq: *A seventeen-year-old nothing trying to make himself important.* Abu Ibrahim hadn't dressed up for Ali's invitation, and he was saying all the wrong things. He said, "Why is this rifle so long, Ali?" He said, "Will it reach all the way to Tripoli?" Ali's cousin began to speak loudly: Aggressors would think twice now before challenging the village of Karaz. Abu Ibrahim kept interrupting: "Explain this to me," he said. "Make me understand." And he said, "Everything you say is nothing. If I worked half as hard as you talk, I'd be a rich man."

Ali's older brother said, "Once again, Abu Ibrahim's talking about how poor he is."

The other men laughed. Abu Ibrahim was a freethinker, someone suggested. How else to explain the small size of his family? Three children. One puny son. Another man said maybe Abu Ibrahim was too smart to want a lot of mouths to feed. Be fair, admonished a third. Abu Ibrahim often tried hard to be a generous man.

Amid laughter, Ali Razzaq squatted in front of Immy. His breath smelled like animal sweat. He clasped Immy's knee with one hand. With his other forefinger, he outlined Immy's foot on the dirt floor. Then he pushed off and stood. Immy stumbled backward, revealing a tiny drawing.

"That, Abu Ibrahim, is your little bridegroom's footprint. The kid's so small he's almost not there. And you talk about 'nothing.'" Immy looked at his feet. He didn't want to be nothing.

In March, the rifle went off in the pathway behind Abu Ibrahim's house. The bullet found the soft filler of mud between two stones, made a hole in the wall, and entered the room in which Abu Ibrahim slept with his family. It came to rest beside the pillow of Umm Ibrahim.

An accident, Ali said. The gun went off while he was loading it. God knew, he would never willingly endanger the family of Abu Ibrahim, whom he loved like a cousin.

In April, war broke out in Beirut.

In July—and August and September—Ali brought gifts from his kitchen garden. Perhaps, he said, these eggplants and cucumbers would help Abu Ibrahim not spend some of the money he earned from driving his taxi. If that were the case, Ali would be content. He wanted only to compensate Abu Ibrahim in any small way he could.

Even Immy, only six years old, understood that Ali's mother and siblings would miss the vegetables. He understood that the family owned no land except the garden. And he understood that people would talk. Abu Ibrahim owned a taxi, they would say. Why should Ali Razzaq shower gifts on a taxi driver? Everyone knew Abu Ibrahim made ten times the money Ali got from farming other people's land. Everyone knew the money the taxi driver didn't spend was piling up somewhere in his house.

Just looking at Ali Razzaq made Immy sick to his stomach. When that seventeen-year-old nothing came to the house with his mouth full of words and his eyes going everywhere and his vegetables tied in a shirt, Immy always remembered the smell of animal sweat and tried to sneak out the window. He escaped a few times, until his mother figured him out. From then on, while Abu Ibrahim sat in the front room with his visitor, Umm Ibrahim kept her hand on Immy's arm. She hissed worry into his ear. It wasn't polite to vanish, she said. Ali Razzaq would think this family had no respect for him. So Immy leaned against his mother and hoped Ali would forget to ask after him. He wanted to stay in the back room with her and his sisters and the big water jar half-full of lira, which she cursed as the source of their troubles.

After each visit, Umm Ibrahim beat her fists on the wall. But she kept her voice down. "We'll never get out before he finds it."

Immy's father would say, "Maybe you want me to be no one in America?" After a moment, he would sigh. "A few more months."

In November, it rained. The rain slammed hard into the village, and the steep pathways between houses turned into rivers. Then the rain stopped. The water ran off, leaving mud. Immy rolled some mud into a pellet and tried to work the pellet into the bullet hole. His mother found him. She grabbed his wrist and squeezed until he let go. She ground the pellet underfoot. It became part of the path again.

Inside, she ranted. "We cannot fix that hole, Immy. No one should even see you looking at that hole. People will tell Ali Razzaq. In no time, we'll have a hundred holes."

That was why the hole was almost a year old on a December night in 1975, when Immy lay in his sheepskins and tried to sleep. A finger of moonlight was wiggling into the house.

He turned over on his side. He closed his eyes. Still, the moon was at his back. It butted and nosed. It burrowed into the soft spot under his shoulder blade. It settled inside him and coiled like a white snake around his lungs.

He sat up, heart charging. His bedding had balled up under his knees. His breathing was loud. For a few minutes, he didn't care if he woke anyone up.

Eventually, he stood. He cared again. He stepped away from the pile of bedding so he wouldn't nudge the sheepskins and make them brush against the floor.

The room breathed around him: His mother's cedar chest, the cooking pots, the large-bellied flour jar, and the two water jars, each as tall as his navel and one of them not what it seemed. All these things had taken on lives of their own. Curves and corners and straight lines—a city of shapes edged in silver by this moon that had been coming to Immy once a month for almost a year.

Since he couldn't do anything about the hole, he would take care of the moon.

The floor felt gritty and cold under his feet. He walked the way Ali's younger brother walked when he was stalking cats. You lowered your heel gently. You made yourself into a woman setting a ceramic bowl down on stone. Then you rolled forward to your toe. Then you lowered the next heel.

One foot in the air, Immy paused in the corner where his sisters slept. Leila was face down, her arms wrapping her head as if she were warding off the moon—and the sun. And her father's measuring eyes, and her mother's irritated glances, and the stream where tomorrow other girls' voices would assess how she washed the family pots, and her own twelve-year-old body, and Immy's curiosity. (She was big and soft, and sometimes he watched her until she hung her head, but when she whispered *please be kind, Immy,* he always relented.)

Hala, only a year younger than her sister, slept masterfully, cramming Leila against the wall. One hand covered the back of Leila's head.

Immy held his breath until the sounds of sleep reassured him. Then he prowled toward the wall where his mother lay beneath a shuttered window. She slept alone.

His father had gone to Beirut yesterday. So, Immy knew, had his father's revolver.

"Why?" Immy had asked as Abu Ibrahim buckled up his suitcase, strapped a holster across his chest, and tucked the revolver into the holster. "Why are you going to Beirut?"

His father grunted. Immy knew what that grunt meant: *Is this boy a baby? Why does he think he can demand answers from me?* Then Abu Ibrahim got into his taxi and drove away.

Immy's mother turned to go inside. "He's going to get passports. That's all, Immy. He'll be back." She briefly leaned one arm on the doorframe. "God willing," she added. *Insha'allah.*

The exhaustion in her voice made Immy run and hide far away from the house. His mother rarely sounded so quiet. When she was in a good mood, she teased, and when she was in a bad mood, she announced her complaints.

When she was in a bad mood, she liked to pick up her broom and run her mind over "the troubles," starting with the Palestinians, who were going to ruin this country. "They can't have Palestine, so now they're getting the whole place in an uproar. Listen, Immy. Sometimes I think they *want* the Israelis to come and destroy us."

Immy would slink to the doorway, thinking *I didn't do it.*

His mother would sweep harder and frown. Finally, she would burst out: "Anyway, the Jews would enjoy killing us. For a while things weren't so good for them. Now they want *us* to suffer." The broom handle would bang against the walls of the house. The dust would rise. She would re-member the Christian militias: "We're not people to them. Any excuse to hunt us down." As the broom knocked around and the dust boiled, Umm Ibrahim would disappear in a whirl of clouds and noise. "Why us, why us? What have we ever done to all these cruel people?"

Immy didn't like loud voices, but noise didn't make the sky close in. What made the sky sit on his head was the helpless look on his mother's face when she stopped in a doorway to say "God willing." That look would return, he knew, if Umm Ibrahim woke to find that Immy was going outside at night, that he was going to walk to a mountaintop and put out the moon.

He'd been to the top once before. But that was in the daytime, with some older boys. For a moment, Immy almost hoped his mother would wake up and ask him why he was standing beside her in the night. She was asleep, though. She was even snoring slightly. He had to go.

On his way out the door, he stopped for his rubber slippers. He carried them past all the houses of the village and didn't put them on until he reached the road to Mishmish. At the big oak tree, he turned off the road. The path took him over rocks and scrub. He passed through a corner of the forest, with its silent pine smell, and emerged into the bright cold of the highest place he knew.

He could look all the way to the sea at El Aabdé. The Mediterranean lay white as ice under the moon, but down there was warmer than here. He knew that. In Tripoli, they had palm trees.

With his hands over his eyes, he tipped his head back. After a long time, he took his hands away. The moon still floated in the night, farther away than before. Immy began to see that the sky was too big to crush him. His relief verged on joy. Land fell away from his feet in every direction, and on the other side of the Mediterranean lay more oceans—more people, too.

His father had gone to Beirut for passports. That meant Immy would see the people on the other side of the world, people whom he pictured crowding down to their beaches, toward the ocean, toward him.

He held his hand up to the sky and blocked out the moon. He let the hand drop, and the moon emerged again. He shouted. His words condensed into a single flutelike note that took off from his mountain, sailed over fruit farms and olive terraces and cities on the coast, wavered, and drifted out to sea.

For a moment, left on his outcropping of stone, Immy wanted to fly after that sound. Silence crowded out of the trees. It crawled up the mountain, the mountain that had made his words into a note. Many words, one note. A note was not nothing, he thought. Then he tried it again. Sentence after sentence rolled up from his stomach. He called out comfort to his mother and urged happiness on his father. He introduced himself to the people he would meet halfway around the world. Each sentence left the mountaintop as a single note, and a part of him traveled with each note. He brushed the leafless twigs of apricot trees. Another part of him shuddered through Ali Razzaq. Another skimmed the carpet in the Beirut apartment where his father was staying the night, and another curled around militiamen at checkpoints, grazing their necks, so that they shivered and looked over their shoulders.

The part of Immy that stayed behind lay down and flung his arms around the stone he'd been standing on. The stone had held up his feet. The night had rained down the air he breathed. He turned onto his back and breathed some more of it.

The descent was easy. He wound back through the woods as if he'd invented the path. He tasted the trees. He mimicked the notes the mountain had made. He tried different pitches and spun them into patterns. As he sang, he bounced down a sloping field of rocks, picking up speed, until he was half running, half falling, down the embankment onto the big road.

The sound of his slippers landing on gravel and the silence that enveloped that sound convinced him. All of it loved him: Behind him, the stands of trees, the hillside he'd just tumbled out of, the night. Before him, the familiar stretch of road leading back to his village, back through the orchards, back down the paths between the houses, and along the stone wall that looked as impersonal as every wall in town—except that on the other side of this wall, his mother slept.

He forgot to hush his footsteps as he passed under the window. His mother's voice cut the air. "Bandits!" He knew she felt the water jar behind her, heavy with lira, like her own belly bared to knives. "Immy, Hala, Leila, where are you? I think I heard bandits!"

Standing beside the shuttered window, Immy began to sing words of reassurance. *Here I am, Mother. I'm not a bandit, I went to see the moon.* He wanted to show his mother what he'd learned, but he surprised even himself. The smell of trees was still lodged in the back of his throat. His lungs and lips were a mountain, rendering whole sentences into single ringing notes. Note after note filled the air. Surely, the entire village would wake.

Instead, his mother stopped shouting. The night sang through Immy, and his voice was a lullaby. Soon he heard her through the shutter, snoring again.

He took off his slippers, laid them down at the front door, and went back to sleep in his spot beneath the bullet hole.

"Almost Nothing Yet the Fragile Amplitude of the World"

—James Sacré

So the aim is all pith and tang and crossing from one body to the next: smell of sweat on the skin a taste of salt and this inner and that outer crossed over through the threshold of touch or of sound: something like poetry, or speech, or music: Monica Peck, Gary Duehr, Timotha Doane, Lisa Rappoport, Susan Thackrey, Christophe Wall-Romana's translation of James Sacré—and a guard against the accidents affecting skin, and touch. The pieces in this section speak to each other oddly, aslant, a lucent haze just nearly forming near the surface of things. The idea of skin as a boundary and of writing as a way through? Entirely too simple. Entirely too much. Dialect, translation, mute photo: something entering in. Hair rises on the back of the neck and air ripples along the skin: an uneasy feeling but a sure one, too: yes, she says, but how did you know? Later, she says: sight unseen.

The child (the essayist Adam Phillips reminds us) must decide to come from silence into language—must actively choose to leave some place behind for another, a choosing as an act of language askew to its own directions: "a skin" something like "askew or "asking"— asking askew with the language we've learned to use to take us to the place of silence. Wanting something more, getting something less: askew. "if other need than hunger / if other sun than fire / she said / would be / a lucidation, a material / fuel fitting flame" (Susan Thackrey). A lingering is in order, all along the way.

What binds us to this world is no more and no less than the shadow of a word held in the air in speech—between two shores, as Lisa Rappoport writes—the sources of light as ever mysterious. The visible skin, the surface, only hints of what's behind or beneath: in gesture, in speaking, in music, in art: we make up the rest in an internal dialect based on the apparent surfaces of the world and their multiple forms of translations. How to tell, who speaks, how, with what twang can I tell if YOU come from Kansas, too, then of MY tribe perhaps, and still another to be marked as presence, present, another being to be understood. In Monica Peck's work, marking the surface as speech with an undertow of geography creates another tongued surface and someone from her life coming into mine—her work "breaking silence"— breaking free, breaking the boundary, marking the break: breaking. There is no going back.

desperate to
reach beyond
this embrace
—TIMOTHA DOANE

Skin the conductor / music the air reverberating in the inner chambers of the ear / special knowledge / an interior sense / whispers on the faces of the dead: "You dare to play Beethoven? See what happens…" : the hand again, as in this section's ending totemic prayer against that hand's harm. The lover's back has "opalescent breadth" (Gary Duehr), a liminal space of reading through touch, resonance unrepealed and breaking through to someplace else: a presence marked by a thousand symbols, as in Timotha Doane's "gridpoem," or a reading meant to be taken from another means of transport—a midwestern twang, an intimation suggested by difference, a repeal from the muteness of the visual into some other art. "Come, Someone Says," the title of Christophe Wall-Romana's wonderful translation of James Sacré. You are there, and I am here: come. I am lost without a place to touch the angle of light that breathes this shadow-speech: or skin. I am lost without the threshold: I am lost without the skin.

—Eileen O Malley Callahan

MONICA PECK

Libation

And then out from behind the house, the stableboy, rein in hand, harness over his shoulders; up
on the ridge, worn out, knees in mud, to fetch
the horse, ornated with rain, hooves pressing
clumps of sea green weeds. Here the fence
and beyond that, the road, in order, also the house, brick draped
with ivy, oatmeal set in bowls on the table—

> still she brushes down the wet horse's hide in the
> stable, avoiding its bared
> teeth and through the slats sees the sky brighten,
> the French woman screwing
> the stable boy, the dogs chewing on rocks in the
> road—

[unable to contain at once all   the fullness
of events names location—

see   this one's face

as he takes—what is unfinished

leave   as such—

unable to finish
open

as taking in   his face

look now—also
ago   as memory   tyranny of the unknown—

she would write letters—never signed—
some never sent—

feeling as if every thought is a bastard
having nothing to travel with

she practices highway robbery]

each event also
[fragment]
what she would love to say if
only she could speak

YES, THE LIGHTS ARE MAKING SPACE

> Walking beneath the bridge and above the water, we
> were lit from below, from the night sky reflected
> on the water. This was just the sort of light.

"I've pissed in lots of rivers, in the daytime, nighttime, near where folks
are passing or way out in the middle of nowhere" she's talking

with ice chips in her cup, fairground mud on her jeans cuffs. "Won't you
sing us something? We want you to just sing! Damn! Anything'll do"

> and they crept up to the edge of the dam overflow, drunk as
> apes in June,

> spendes o dionysios

spende   pouring Early Times into the Kansas river

> in the woods, later, losing their minds and guts behind a moss-
> covered stone and she:

> "See them lights there, just there? That's a cruising spot for

And he   "Naw, I thought that was up at the camponileee

leaning against the rock, smoking cigarettes, each imagines johns
> fetching their nightly sort

> "Thems always tryin' to get into mah pants!"

> and so she's got her hand inside his jeans and he's lying on his back

on the wet
ground groaning something about

"gettin' satlights out there to count all them fucking starz—
count them all—the slew of 'em"

lying there, elbow propped so it's sticking into the mud

     she's wandered off, singing

          well the doorknob keeps on turning
          I think there's spooks a-round mah bed

—THEN Madame Rose (the French woman) comes, legs bared to the
Welsh dawn, stableboy turning his head and curses, seeing the fourteen-
yr-old's eyes staring back and Madame Rose
is saying

      "gutavwa gutavwa gutavwa

             The damned horse bites the fourteen-yr-old's
                shoulder, sending her out,
             past the dogs chewing on rocks into the house
                frost still on the grass, to the
             kitchen where they've all gathered to eat—she's
                the last one—since her
             horse is white and meaner'n a stick

Instances

Looking down the alley, northward, towards the river, as if there's a giant
down there waiting, standing behind that house; I am waiting for her

her absence   :   the giant

        beyond those buildings

        perhaps she will

        arrive from   the way her hands are aether

                nutmeg, oranges, black tea.

she does not remember the stone—what it was—only that it was worn in
    a place and when

    will she turn so the back of her neck—wanting
    at that point what is not allowed—

how will the others be told   what it is to be errant   that this is the place
                                    of aberrance
or her turning   the smell of almonds and linseed

the acorn squash that this room was painted from or the tropical papaw
placing her hand against the streak of gray, just there

fear of the talk, as a result of

wanting instead: her and also
                      the persimmon tree, fruit laden.

Seeing the consequence, the following with
as the curve of her lip, red leaf of orange leaf
walking on the brick sidewalk, leaves
on the ground, pasted

If only to comment on this—and the thin yellow of illumined beer,
      collared with white
turning the corner in the afternoon
from the eyes of Jorge sweeping the alley, red handkerchief around
      his neck,
or what the man in the car, would think—to hear:

                what she would love to do when arriving
                and seeing her eyes.

The threshold of season.

Here is the trope:

what the mind does towards her towards her turning   her ether here

in the face of events   of a circus

sawdust, striped cloth   ropes, chairs   the bending
of animals

of the beasts   in their faces

in the face of rigidity   feelings as treason   betrayal of
others'

wanting   in the event of a surface.

Her language is the paint; the fear of losing

of blunders   of lack

when was it   she was a child   her first, taking off clothes in the dark,
the turning of the sky, the sheets of the clouds of the next threshold of
          sound of skin to air

lip : breath : smoke, the fumes of errands—   search for

the tools of searching   to the words, what each thing chooses

not to be hair or skin, but eye.

GARY DUEHR

Tangent

Crossing through the house, naked, in the blue light
After dawn, you imagine this is how those who've just died

Must try to keep measure of things. Out in
Back, rainwater drips on tin. You find yourself fully

Awake, more so than during the day; past guilts
Rush up inside you the way blood can surge unexpectedly

To the face and fingertips, giving off a certain
Buzz of knowingness—only to diffuse into a joy

At being here in this place, this doorway, at this
Exact time: the light lies down on the surface

Of the coffee table, the rug, the pavement. No birds. Only
The dull roar of machinery, a car ratcheting past.

Soon you will return to where the sheet
Has fallen from your lover's bare back, its opalescent breadth

Curving all the way back into your dream.

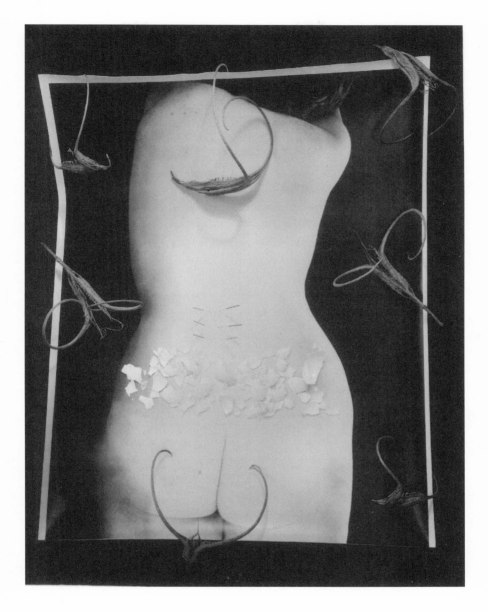

LISA RAPPOPORT, *Back Trouble*, photograph, 14"x 11", 1986

On Mortality

In da Vinci's last years, an apocalyptic storm came obsessively
To mind: how great elms surgically remove
Even their slenderest shoots from shaken, clumped dirt;
How inky clouds whirl ever tighter in a cartoon
Of disaster, the air a tincture of rust mixed with mortality's
Cyan—the color of the lips
Of the drowned, of shadowy dug-out pockets in snow.
Still, those around him reclined tamely, and when the time came
Parted their skin along one long incision
So he could write helpful marginalia across their tracts and systems
As if on a water-stained map
For the next set of weary travelers.

LISA RAPPOPORT

Fire, Milk, Blood

Nothing is like a sorrel horse against new snow,
perfect balance of intensities, unless
that even more intense flood of rippling color,
a fire burning in the snow, starting to melt
through the permeable surface.

His skin had the feel of milk—
or it felt how milk looks—
thick, opaque, smooth.
Not impenetrable: I saw his thumb
torn by a door, the flesh edging the nail
stripped loose, the wine-dark blood
dripping, not fast, not slow,
like sap drips from a drilled tree.
Smooth and cool, his skin,
ready to be shed.

Before, there was that other fire,
that other flood of color:
Blood spurting onto snow
from the leg of a horse
caught by the teeth
of a barbed wire fence
buried beneath a drift—
flying blood, fluid heat
blooming on frozen white ground,
passion flowers about to drop or drown.

Navigation

A moment of a garden
is what you told me, a moment
of flowered green air perched
above the bay, clinging in tiers onto
the steep incline. Now boats move below,
heartbeats on the moving water, lights, means
of arrival or of escape. From here all falls away,
rushing down in the night. What tentative ligatures
clasp us to this earth. We navigate with radar,
faith, heat-seeking devices. Make lives
where fate deposits us. Keep the fires burning. Ships
bear lanterns to signal their whereabouts: approaching,
you know their bulk lies to the right of red, to the left
of green. Floating homes, moored or unmoored, skimming
the thin membrane of separation. So much remains
below water—barnacles, slowly widening cracks,
unknown threats. A sailor trusts in buoyancy. On land
gravity is salvation. There are only two shores:
The lamp we light in the dark morning,
the other lamp we light at dusk.

TIMOTHA DOANE

The Pregnant Moon

It is said that the moon
stores all images
It is said that the moon
drives us mad
in love or war or loneliness

Her weight has indeed blessed
                              or cursed
every form
visited on Earth
resides in the light
of that body
pockmarked by time

She gives birth
and we believe
enough
to create truth
x-rated nationhood
dangerous and
full of pain

rising on the smoke
we make offerings
desperate to
reach beyond
this embrace

Earth holds the moon
the moon
          our intimate

not like the polygamous sun
with relations everywhere
in the Universe

threads between bodies are light
Ariadne shows us
through the maze
of our own making

there
in the give and take
tides of Tonglen
our teacher beams on us
sitting next to the vulture
                       corpse eater
the moon

cheetahs will not eat
the dead
lions take only a fresh Buddha
they are of the sun
               golden butterfly
               and
               hot rocks

What grid is this
laid on life?

Marilyn joins the women
eight thousand years of mourning
while a red and a white dragon
fight
on the jade mandala

green snakes
issue from the green man's
moon mask for Pharaoh

Malcolm X, like Ariadne,
threads the maze
lamp
out of the spawn of lies

Saints and dualities
go up in spoke
amphibians
and green eyed Amazonian cats
on the edge of extinction
tell us our result

Election Pantoum

The nation turns on a savage thing
a dead heat neck and neck
dancing numbers tease the same
hearts that climb phantom mountains

a dead heat neck and neck
where is the exit on this freeway?
hearts that climb phantom mountains
never grow vines for hummingbirds

where is the exit on this freeway?
what's at stake, her date inquired?
never grow vines for hummingbirds
slow to a pace of dead reckoning

what's at stake, her date inquired?
the inevitable replay of times' doodling
slow to a pace of dead reckoning
visibility is bad, calculate the state's position

the inevitable replay of time's doodling
skulls roll, the brothers are in control
visibility is bad, calculate the state's position
nobody said this was Gemini's time

skulls roll, the brothers are in control
felony count. Don't need to get snippy
nobody said this was Gemini's time
death warrants and Texas yippee

dancing numbers tease the same
nation turns on a savage thing

SUSAN THACKREY

from *Lyre*

1.

punishment wide
as a life some
stellar virulence
propounded day
by day
keelhauled and
shell by shell
undertow prevails
set sail
fifty companions brave and boisterous
fare in disgrace bereaved
of light surveilled
of fifty stories shunned
by dark a
sundering a
surface

2.

across the face of
some world
surface mars
original sea
put a face on it
unbearable autopsy
as (no) sinews string
the false anatomy
no gut uncoils to serpent
edible flesh
unfit for consumption
slice of life in
eden eating was all
king cannibal

3.

premised in place
of promise
corpse in the copse
some trees, a wood
mystery lightens
shred of evidence burden
of proof hangs
in the balance broken
beam restored by
force fell on
hard times
"approach the bar with caution"
judgement is not justice given
exhibits "A" and "B"

4.

mineral planet
important portions of green
mecanique celeste
running in place
impatient placements of green
granite metamorph
no need for
that hypothesis
extremely precarious
event

5.

light is what is
burned
as star as flesh
goes
out hunting bow and
arrow in
the center of
the splintered
   wood a-hunting go
incurring flame
eyes enrolled toward
it is
necessary this
takes place only
world entropical
striking
similarity
end vision like
end game
bird in
burning flight
thousand tongues of
tropics veers toward
version
of crux of crucible
   if other need than hunger
   if other sun than fire
   she said
   would be
   a lucidation, a material
   fuel fitting flame

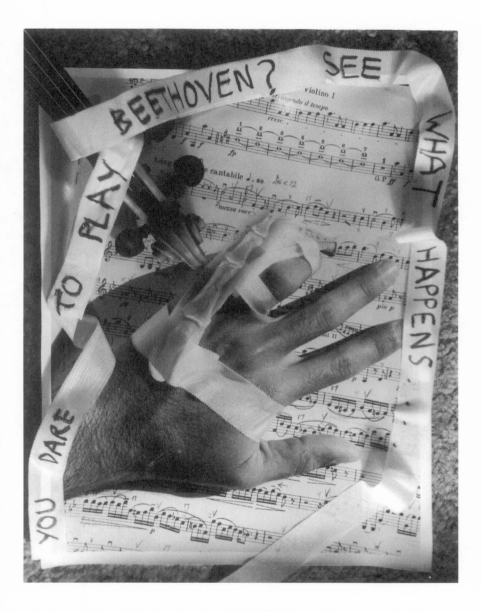

LISA RAPPOPORT, *Dare to Play Beethoven*, photograph, 14"x 11", 1986

from *Come, Someone Says*

In the voice that says come, as in those cadences akin to moments of listening, there is often the written word of Jillali Echarradi.

Perhaps in order to reach with words into something like a landscape, perhaps a certain vocabulary ought to be chosen and sentences put together so as to give the reader's body—with startled eyes, with nostrils that dilate in the light stretching into the very far—the impression that it is about to move forward a bit more—hillock of cropped alfalfa under the few olive trees—in order to lose itself into space—the feel of being carried away, but as if through a beautiful indifference, by the world unfolding its paradise just ahead.

At the time you're writing you know perfectly well that it might be better not to speak of the difficulties you encounter in choosing (yes, the term doesn't really fit) your words.

Yet beforehand (in another poem) I waited a long time for a way to come about in turning a few articles so the sentence would be brighter (with my desire busy with a landscape no more exact actually than a smile can be); I am now of a mind that the attention paid to such minuscule ponderings of grammatical forms is no less necessary to the impression the poem gives than noticing in the distance (and as if my reflection was another way of moving my body forward under the foliage of the olive trees) the almost imperceptible motion of a peasant's progress over the faint ordering of cultures.

Cadence 1

The town shines from afar like a gilded ring in the raised hand of a woman.

To see this you must come from the right direction and not just at any time. To see it with greater contentment you must go to town for no reason whatsoever and even be able to think you're going nowhere

Because in a while the town will have the look of an abandoned town on account of the flattened cardboard in front of shops, on account of discarded produce, at night, when you cross the empty market. And rain coming from time to time.

One day you sit down at the terrace of a cafe to talk about it with a friend. Without reaching any conclusion, nor even being sure that you said anything true. Or worthy.

Later you imagine you see the words in a poem shine.

You're at the terrace of a cafe, or sometimes in a small courtyard after having gone through the main room jammed with vacated chairs all of them turned to the television that gives off a noise of music and political patter in a corner, you're there as if invited into someone's home. Orange-colored chairs and a fig tree with a sweet smell, under which we've now sat ourselves. Adjacent to this narrow space more broken chairs create a slight disarray, same orange color, and rusted metallic frames, weeds, some pieces of wood.

You stay there quite a while—not because you're trying to understand. It's more like there's nothing to understand. You may even think that here you are wasting your time and that there would be many more useful things to do. Such as writing for instance. Seriously writing: there would be a whole row of dictionaries in front of you on a long comfortable table and nearby in the room used as a library, some carefully ordered documentation on the customs of this land (no doubt looking into it carefully you would find what there is to know of the Ksar el Kebir cafes, and even an explanation of why I find myself there. I haven't seen any other European in town, for the few days I've been here).

Writing to understand better?

If I recall correctly it was just a nice moment in that back courtyard like a quiet corner in a country dive (familiar to me because of the mishmash of sweet-smelling tree and old stuff tossed as if along the side of a barn). We tried with the friend who brought me there (yes, as if into his home) explaining to ourselves something of our ways of being together—and this was but one more way. What mattered, so it seemed to me, was the light (thinner on account of the mint tea in the glasses) and the scent of the fig tree. All the same we ended up leaving.

This was a while back already. Now I am writing. Yes, I did need to pick up a dictionary and verify the meaning of a word. A French word to talk about a Moroccan cafe in Ksar el Kebir. Yes, I sense this poem is finished and the friend will smile: I said nothing—or so little.

It may well be the most abandoned place in the whole country. Someone from town is taking me over there. From the top of a minaret he showed me where it was, almost outside of town, beyond a small Jewish building. The cypresses can be seen from pretty far.

The town is very old, but you kind of put it out of your head— itself, it seems, is letting its old Portuguese towers go,

Together with a small cluster of vats and ponds for tanners . . . and within the other side of its length, Spanish drinking troughs for horses.

We walked for a long time

And saw for instance graveyards, where people keep abandoning their bodies to the ground, with little vanity about the graves, a lot of very tall grass we barely see where we're going, amid a few trees, and old stuff discarded. Perhaps it is because the administration in charge of cemeteries and holy places doesn't do its job. But isn't this manner of abandoning corpses more touching than when graves are too well-kept?

And when we arrived to this former colonial cemetery, among its broken headstones (and some of the cypresses too), the earth of the place all torn up, and sometimes a bone, then you understood even better that cemeteries are useless and, above all, that they do not speak of eternity.

It isn't far from this town that Jean Genet wanted to be buried. In a Spanish cemetery also and when I went to Larrache I only visited Arab graveyards which form a beautiful place up high on the seashore. Maybe we ran out of time to go see the Spanish cemetery. I assume Jean Genet didn't know the one in Ksar el Kebir: I know of no place more forlorn, more forgotten. I guess he got it wrong, it is there he should have offered his body, never to give another thought, to time. But that's the point— here or elsewhere, it doesn't matter.

Someone took me into these landscapes. Come, his voice says adding at times syllables of a first name. Come! And the journey is just as much in the fields, or places in town, as in the friendship of this voice.

Come. And it is for instance in-between a village like nowhere (the infinite sky, its houses you can't see within enclosures of cactus) and the far-off line of a forest it is in a great meadow space that leads all the way to hills where the green color of grass goes on. You pass through with your own silence, and any anxiety you might have finds a rest because of the feeling of being at last there alone while discovering at the same time a plentiful presence, and something of life that keeps company without saying one thing too many; people, animals, as if the air and color of the landscape. Almost nothing yet the fragile span of the world.

When you get to the forest I'd like it to be as if on the edge of a new poem. Come (I can hear the noise of any other first name inside mine).

In some way you would like to hasten the writing of the book, as if too much waiting threatened with oblivion many things that already make up its presence within the desire you have to write it.

But you know full well that you'll have to finish the book, that you will one day leave it for another: then you imagine going slowly, for a long time. Waiting

May well be in order to carry better within yourself and into words
What you're forgetting among what you don't forget.

You cannot know.

The book will be made of these hasty raptures of desire
Together with the fear of moving too fast through all that is going to re-main in silence.

Nothing too bad, if truth be said. The plain recognition that you don't know how a book is supposed to be written. Probably because you don't know much better

What it wants to be used for.

A book like some time you're about to spend with the word living
In the shadow of the word dying

You can say it all the voice said;
And all you were going to say
Has already been said. There's nothing more
Than the coming of time. More time
Coming.

Translated from French by Christophe Wall-Romana

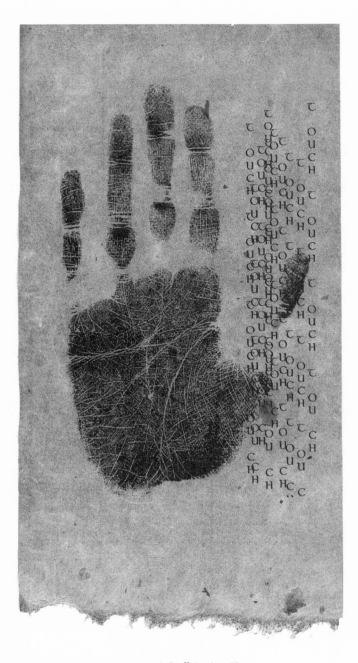

EILEEN O MALLEY CALLAHAN, *A Spell Against Harm*,
laser print on rice paper, 8½"x 4½", 2000

JENIE PAK

Emergency Room

My arm bruises from the tetanus shot,
Won't be touched. The finger I cut
Deep, stitched up, reconciles.
Nothing but time, looking into glass bowls—
Reflect armor, speaking wild bright something;

Empty what is unwanted from this body,
Incinerate. Soon, the scent of leaves burning
Will be a second coat. Strip the bark,
Let sap run. Blood keeps surfacing,
Toxins wash like dreams, watch smoke rise.

Soon, skin will chill to memory
Unidentified, nothing to press tongues upon.
Was it some night like this, crickets carving blank faces?
Not a smile, not one jewelled eye
Pushing its crocodile blister through my mind;

Paint and paint a lacquer of cells:
Go by amaranth, indigo, meadow,
Colors not imagined; put on a show.
Whatever the gallery, is absence
And whatever the season, it will pass—

There are other kinds of brilliance.
I don't mean stars, planets, moments like these
Where I can't focus on a single thing. And I am
Loving dumbness, pleasure, anticipating the clematis;
Crowding, now, into its singular virgin shell.

Red Sorghum

Dear Skeleton of the Great Blue Whale:

You hang from the museum ceiling, we *ooh*
And *ahh,* our breaths winding through your ribs.
Don't tell me you don't want to be here, up there,
Your wrecked body suspended, exposed for all the world to see.
Don't insist on a proper burial where you swim through fire,
Devour a sand of ashes. See my open mouth: good for words
And eating. But you are useless, pulled from the beach—
A genie from its bottle made deaf to wishes, demagnetized by the sea.

Dear Absent Clone of Myself:

Where are you? I examine microscopic slides, look for the irregular
You. What's invading what? Cells, burst or swollen,
Bumping into each other, drifting, drifting apart.
Picasso's women: Are you them? Are you me?
Am I? Are you the happy ghost under PQ 7558C, every staticky channel
    on TV.
Are you the Shivaitic androgyne, nothing and all?

Dear Invisible Philosophical Friend:

Do you remember the guy who could bend spoons with his mind?
What seductive chaos. Was it silver, his mind?
And who needs a body with powers like that?
Remember the foreign film we saw? The man who had to
Skin his friend alive, or die? All this, remember, while nearby,
The sorghum that would be used for wine, swayed drowsy in the
    breeze—
Seeing nothing when the wrist hesitated, their flimsy limbs touching,
As the body bled, staining the blade
Carving into the skin, its unstoppable singing.

H. E. FRANCIS

Anchorwoman

There she was, the anchorwoman, smiling professionally at the world. Her face on the six and ten o'clock news never failed to excite him. In old movies he'd seen stars with teeth like hers, Gene Tierney and Gloria Grahame. The sight of her prominent upper teeth made the lover feel them barely brush his lips. He'd become too susceptible. He knew what those teeth led to: *You* know the one I'm secretly smiling at. Her voice silk was on his skin; and her teeth, he could run his tongue over them, under. The news was on that lawyer again. Since the young lawyer's case, she hardly had time for food, drink, sex, time with him. What am I for if not work? She'd smile, kiss, give a love tap. When this case is over, I'll go for yours— all the way. Over? She was day and night on it, in and out of the TV van, hoofing it with the camera crew and waiting *hours*, though as the anchorwoman she didn't have to. But this story she was really going after. It was a first. Anything could come of it for her and the station and the area. What am *I* for if not work? And when she *did* come in, she was endlessly on the phone or changing outfits for the six and ten.

The reporter admired the anchorwoman, identified with her, at least with her tenacity, reflecting his own. Her casual presentation cloaked a fierce concentration. She had spent time at his office, because the divorcee had called him first: I know your stories, how you work. The divorcee had called confidentially. She would have no meeting in his office but at her house because she had children, two. An exclusive, he suspected. Headlines. Ordinary, the divorcee: dark hair and eyes, middling tall, not unattractive but nothing to call attention to her, in fact the slightest sloppiness in her middle, and hips; but intelligent, a tech editor, who talked well (Had that been her initial appeal to the lawyer?) and had laid bare her *situation*. The young lawyer claimed he had had no sign of infection when he had met the divorcee (timing would come to be the crux of the matter). In the telling the divorcee was not agitated; her control was proof of her intelligence. She, who had been abstinent since her divorce, had met the young lawyer at a party given by friends, the young lawyer no doubt invited especially to meet her. Her friends worried about her always at work or with the children, having no other life. And it had worked, her friends knew. You trust your friends. You do? the reporter said. Don't *you?* she said. Silent, the reporter waited for her to continue. So the affair had gone on for a couple of years now. She had trusted the lawyer until her medical exam: she had become infected, and from whom? Who else! You can imagine my reaction! But the reporter said Tell me. And she: At the moment the doctor told me, I asked *Are you certain?* and at his *Yes* I could have struck, killed with my bare hands. I thought *Impossible.* In the confusion of fury I thought *dying,* I thought *my kids, that liar lying to me,* I thought *my job, future.* The reporter interrupted: And you came to me to tell your story because . . .? To get the truth out, show what can happen in sex, warn people of what they could be getting into. She had a teacher's impulse. I go along with all that, the reporter said, but waiting. The hiatus was so long he finally said You've gone to a lawyer? Oh, yes. Then you're suing? Yes. For the kids' future. What will they do if I die, or if they . . . It takes sometimes years to show up in tests. He knew she didn't want to say the worst. He sympathized. *He* had kids to think of. And your lawyer— What's he think of your coming to me? He doesn't know, but he can't object. It will strengthen his case for me and the kids. He's taken the case on contingency because it will make a precedent. The reporter had the divorcee on tape. He had gone over and over the young lawyer and the divorcee's known history. He'd laid it out for his editor, who was excited over the scoop, an unfortunate situation but vital to be told, so page one headlines. For days, with each development, the reporter kept the closest tabs on each new fact and nuance, right on the tail of his now near companion in arms, the anchorwoman.

If the anchorwoman's body was agile and precise in its movements, on hiring no one could have predicted the agility and precision of her mind, what the brilliant college freshman in graphics had whispered (she'd heard him and without batting a lash) was her extraordinary "ratiocination." She went straight at digging the truth out—like you, she assured the divorcee. She'd seen her twice. They had become friendly, if not exactly friends, because the anchorwoman couldn't let her emotions color the way she saw the divorcee. She must not for a moment let her mind slip from "the cause," infection, and all its possible future ramifications; not let the case descend to a mere human interest story. If it was certainly that to a good many readers, to others it was part of a shared effort to expose sin, perversity, babylon. So, as charming yet as objective as she could be, she faithfully went at the divorcee with the fundamental questions: Is there medical evidence? Did you know from the beginning? At what point did you find out? Why didn't he tell you at once? And the anchorwoman tried to discover from the young lawyer's doctor if he had had tests, had known, before he began a relationship with the divorcee or if the infection had become evident later in their affair. But the doctor insisted on respecting the privacy of his patient. After, she had had one, only one, interview with the young lawyer. Surely not yet aware that the bomb was about to explode, he too had insisted on privacy. It was not only his right but her duty to respect it. He said he was sure that under circumstances so emotional, the divorcee had no doubt created some confusion about their situation. The anchorwoman was sorry about the confusion. She would be glad to return when the divorcee had clarified things less emotionally. Then the anchorwoman would be glad to clarify what truth the doctor and the young lawyer might be willing to share with the public now that the situation was no longer (she almost said "a sleeping dog") private.

Lied, the divorcee said. He *had*. Stared me straight in the eye and said Honest, I didn't know. Then how could *I* test positive? she'd asked. I've never slept with any man since my divorce, never. You don't *believe* that? Why should I lie to you when you're lying to *me*. You have to be. There's no other way it could have come to me but through you, and you say *Nobody else,* but how far back *nobody?* But how many then? And what kind of women? You don't tell me that. *Nothing* you tell me. How *could* you betray me, the kids, my friends, and yourself! My husband, you say? How *could* he during *our* relationship? Before? There was no epidemic, no rage of it, when I married him. You! And me thinking This is the straight guy. Maybe after all this, marriage. Maybe the kids will have the right man's influence. The divorcee had a thousand times gone over it—at first, home from the doctor, the shock and stun; and then the rage, striking things, hours of fury at *him,* at *his* shock and stun; then at the lies, his lying. Then came her long meditations. How could she be sure of her impulses and

motives? She told herself she was sure it was not only hurt, pride, disillu-
sion, fear, fury, vengeance, a hate the instant reversal of love. All finally
sieved down to justice, truth, and a warning to others through her mis-
take. No, not money, though she had to think of the kids' future. What
would the poor kids do if she were down, weak, helpless? She counted on
a community sympathetic to anyone in her situation, on an area with a
heavy biblical cornerstone and moneyed with a strongly protective
Chamber of Commerce and aware of its always possible political impor-
tance on the national scene. How could she remain silent? So she had
called the paper and asked for the reporter. Then she was inundated with
calls from lawyers anxious to handle the case—on contingency, of course.
I have a lawyer, she said.

The young lawyer saw himself on TV. It startled. He was running. He
had never seen himself live on camera. Running. Running from the cameras. The man ran from the house to the car and slid in and locked the
door. The man ran from his car to his office and slammed the door. He
had never seen himself side to, never seen himself from behind. He was a
stranger to himself. He looked small. He'd never thought of himself as
that small. Bent over. And skulking. Making a dash for it. From the house
to the car. From the car to the office. They played the tapes at six a.m. and
ten a.m., at six p.m and ten p.m, at six/ten, six/ten, six/ten. They replayed
with each new minute revelation in the young lawyer's relationship with
the divorcee. Running. He saw it so often he could not imagine himself
not running—that young man he had never thought of as small, skulking, running; that young man whom he had maybe never even known,
seen from a perspective he might never have imagined. He imagined the
viewers seeing only that young man, no other, that young lawyer infected,
infecting a divorcee, small, looking cowardly, running like a shamed
criminal, silent, evading reporters and cameramen, aware that he might
never stop running and that there would be no other image of him but
that one permanently on tape, confined in their minds, running from
cameramen, journalists, the public; running from her. Running from you,
he said to the TV. Running from myself, he said aloud. And to myself. I'm
running to myself, the young lawyer said.

The reporter had regular meetings with the divorcee. She would talk to no one but him and her lawyer. She trusted the reporter, knowing he would relay accurate information to the anchorwoman. Fine. That furthered her cause: but the divorcee drew the line, no photos because of the children. Keep them out of this. And no photos of the divorcee did appear in the papers. She was not anonymous. Her name was in print, the city knew it now, but she had miraculously kept herself undercover. The crux was the doctor's files. The young lawyer claimed he was clean when he and the divorcee had met. If, as she claimed, her infection could have come from no one else, then at some point in their relationship he knew and did not tell her. He denied having been infected from the beginning, and after she had told him she was infected, *he* had gone to his doctor. Was it possible that it could have come from an earlier relationship on *her* part? Earlier affair? Insult on insult. She was a mother with two children. She had had to be careful. Careful. And hadn't her infection shown later than his? Hadn't it? Then you know what to conclude from that. Her lawyer said she had a ninety-nine percent chance of winning the case. I have to because of the children. What will they do when I'm finally down, or die? People should be warned that unsafe sex could mean death. Her lawyer said He hasn't a chance, the paper and television have done good exposés, and you've certainly got the public on your side. I should have, she said. Nobody has the right to lie and hurt others and get away with it, nobody.

The divorcee had had it out with the young lawyer—the crucial, ultimate round, the break. If you cared, he said, we could live together, get married. Get married, infected? She was horrified. Why not? We've *been* satisfied, haven't we? We've been happy. Who gets along better? And it's safest for both of us. We can't change things. Being a carrier doesn't necessarily mean destruction. Live with a liar, she said, all my life with a liar, and my children with a liar? And he: How'd I *know* I was lying? I didn't know it until you became a carrier and then *I* saw my doctor and then he verified. Verified what you did know but concealed, she said. No, no. Then why the doctor's reluctance? Because it's his obligation not to reveal private— Private! she cried. It's now a public case. Besides, you're a lawyer, you know better—it's a matter of justice. And your will, he said. My will? Yes. You chose me. You said yes to me. That makes us both responsible. I didn't know *what* I was saying yes to. Most people don't, he said. That doesn't release you from responsibility. Or you, he said. Don't excuse yourself, she said. Don't you, he said. The divorcee had said nothing to him about suing. After, she had called a lawyer. About a confidential matter, which I can't mention over the phone, she had said.

Running. Christ, the lover said, look at him. If they played it backwards, he'd be as comical as Charlie Chaplin. Well, it's *not* funny, the anchorwoman said, the divorcee's a wreck. From what I see, so's the young lawyer, the lover said, and *you'll* be if you don't let up. She had stopped by his place, so he knew she needed release. *She'd* never admit that. She needed an affirmation of herself off the air to bolster her view of the woman on the air. Surely she would be appalled if he actually uttered that. There were truths, he knew from long experience with women, that you simply did not utter. With her any question of reverse dependence was strictly verboten. She would laugh it off as false. Now, a quickie. She chafed till *unbearable.* She mounted—*Don't, don't move*—moving with fierce concentration in tortuous rhythm. She took him, yes, took. No woman had ever driven him to cry out with her like this. He could not stop his hands over her. Her body urged. Spend the night, he said. Not until your divorce comes through, she said. Then you can make an honest woman of me. She laughed. See you on the news. Was the tantalizing part that these moments were so quickly over that they seemed illusory? What excited was how his mind could strip her of the public facade, penetrate it. He knew the promise and the substance. What excited most was that he was certain only he knew what fires were in her.

The young lawyer knew walls now. At home. *Enclosed.* The world shrank. The office—with his two colleagues and the secretary—was tarnished. He had spilled an aura of notoriety over them. Most clients had immediately cancelled all connection. Some kept appointments (which the first two days *he* had kept; then, hounded, he hid at home and worked out of his study, called from there, usually to cancel or postpone). A few called to tell of their support: *that* was irrelevant, his affair not theirs. He made no visits. His mother and father came to his place. *We're behind you, son. It's unfortunate but done.* But *she,* whom he had wanted but could not want now, did not come. Still he wanted to make her understand his guilty innocence or innocent guilt. The infection—as perverse as this might sound to her—could have been the disguised blessing which made them realize love real and forgiving and eased them into marriage. He failed. And she. What this confusion called a lie! Was there a *just* lie? Ethics, profession, love, life itself were on the line. Running. He could not escape the image of himself running. Night he could not sleep, day not work. Wherever he looked, he saw that young lawyer running, running over his eyes, over his table furniture walls windows trees street. He was dragging his life like a dirty rag tied to a dog's tail for all the world to see. *Running.* What he was running from was invisible, and he could not see what he was running toward. Ahead was blank as sky. Nothing.

The reporter and his photographer kept watch at the young lawyer's house. The TV newsmen parked their vans close by, alert for any movement, wanting firsts. The anchorwoman kept in close contact with the reporter. Aces from the TV stations invaded the newspaper offices, coveting coverage of the young lawyer's or the divorcee's "on scene" moves, observing who came, who went, what was going on inside the houses and the office. They tried to hustle interviews with anyone connected with the young lawyer. The reporter was a presence. He wanted truth, though in his most honest moments he felt the evasiveness of that concept and of what it might be based on, yet he could not help theorizing about the relationship between facts and his conclusions about human conduct, which naturally reflected the moral life of society. To him, the moral life consisted of standards which allowed people of different ideas and beliefs to live in mutually beneficial harmony. His view was practical, not religious. In his thinking there was an intimate relation between rational conduct and the irrational impulse which was always a challenge to reason. Ironically, it *sharpened* reason. And cases which sharply focused on that relationship—and the young lawyer's was one—were his primary fascination. He would give anything to talk to the young lawyer. The young lawyer had had everything going for him—graduated the top of his class, gone into an office with two first-rate lawyers, moved right into the city's legal scene. Then under the guise of what—chance? nature? error?—disharmony erupted. That chaos instantly alerted a host of forces—the reporter was one—of social salvation, of reason. He could not miss this chance at a major story with prime reverberations for society, stuff for the front page, where the paper kept it day after day relentlessly.

The young lawyer thought relentlessly. There was, increasingly, little else he could do since he had ceased going to the office. His immediate problem was how to avoid *them,* the media vultures, hovering, intruding with camera bursts of light, driving him into his cave. At least he had the phone, his subterranean salvation. But the walls grew tight. Space suffocated. His problem with the divorcee—intimacy, sex, love—sank below the problem of infection, his and hers. The doctor had said that, though they were carriers, there was no assurance that the symptoms might never develop into a full-blown, life-threatening infection. But both those problems—the divorcee and disease—at the moment sank below the immediate matter, work. Work was salvation, work was the order of life, his and hers, of life itself. But *no* work now. And *why* no work? Because the divorcee had not gone merely to a lawyer—fine, right, just—but why also to the newspaper? Because she had insisted on getting to the heart of the matter, and the matter was beyond the relationship between the two of them. Vengeance she had claimed was no motive, though naturally she was deeply hurt. No, her obligation was to reveal the tragic dilemma of irresponsible sex and, in this case, of lying—yes, lying. And yes, she had thought it all out—for her children's and the social good. No, money was not primary, though of *course* she had to think of money. Who wouldn't? After all, she had the children to support and their future to think of. Her emotion was logical in her situation, the young lawyer thought. His own was. But she had thought it all out under emotion. Surely she believed, since her reasons were so logical, that reason alone was acting. And of *course* reason over emotion was right. Was it always? If so, then, wouldn't the proof be that, instead of making a public display of irrationality couched in terms of reason, she quell her emotions long enough to see that true reason would require them to discuss the matter and make a reasonable and private settlement between them? But, no. She had tossed him and herself to the public, and the public had chomped the case to bits. The public was no more concerned about *her* than it was about *him.* No. People were concerned about their opinions. The case fed them fodder. Not the law, not the doctor, not the divorcee, not the media had been able to define or further with clarity a fundamental and reasonable purpose for exposing the case, which was causing such a polemic. Continued coverage made it *live* because there was a victim infected, identified, isolated, and there was a culprit infected, identified, isolated.

Because the case is a first here, the anchorwoman said. For the station or—? the lover asked. Don't be snide! For the station, me, the city. More. The judicial result just *may* create a precedent and eventually save lives. Anything to keep people from leaping without thinking into licentious sex is no small matter. Yes, he said, sex and thinking always go hand in hand. You! But *yes,* they should. You just wait, he said, till after the banquet. She was quivering. Cool at work, she seldom showed excitement. But tonight was *her* night at the Hilton. *The* anchorwoman. Voted best in the state. For the year's work. Her first. And now, with the divorcee's case in all the state papers . . . Proof that you had to burrow, and unceasingly, like any professional researcher going after a virus, DNA, whatever, or any MD with a scalpel, or any lawyer . . . The quality of your work was who you were. Keep the quality up at any cost. You gave. And society gave the nod. At times she thought about an eventual move to New Orleans, St. Louis, Chicago, L.A., New York . . . Tonight the public would see her as the object. What would family, friends, and teachers at home think of her award? They'd see it at ten. Her lover would be there, sitting discreetly with others, careful because of the Station and because of his pending divorce, though their romance was no secret. Tonight, while at the Hilton, she would depend on her assistants and the reporter. Associates they had become despite competition between the paper and the several TV stations. For two weeks not once had they let up. The case captured readers because the subject was hot. It was contentious because it involved health, family, religion, science, politics, and the very basis of life, sex. Parking at the Hilton the lover leaned over to kiss— Don't! My makeup, she said. Later, she said. Later? She'd rush right off to that young lawyer's house after the banquet. Then she asked Would you go *anywhere* with me? She smiled those sexy teeth. Where might that be? he asked. Anywhere, she said. He smiled. I know you will if the time ever comes, she said.

Enclosed. Had the divorcee thought of that? What good could he do her or her children confined to the walls of his apartment so that he had to sneak out the back way or have a friend or his brother hustle him out? Compensation she wanted. He had no money but the imagined future money his work might bring in. Did she want to attach that? Well, how make it? She had cut him off. His very confinement was evidence that she had deluded herself by thinking that she was being logical. She wanted to attach his earnings but had cut him off from earning. Dialogue. He had wanted dialogue. Naturally she had attacked him and on moral grounds, but she had resisted dialogue, dialogue as he knew it. Without a word to him she had gone legal. And now *he* would like to have a legal arrangement. She had, yes, called his hand and forced him to that desire—too late. She had set in motion the action of law. But he was involved in something more than a legal action. What he was experiencing, and what confounded, was justice as he had never known it. When he saw that man, himself, running, he saw with fascination and horror the motion of something making that man run; and that motion would not stop— could it?—even after he had stopped running. But *when* had that motion really started? How far back? Before he and the divorcee had met? Before her discovery of the infection, and his? Before his youth? Before birth? Sitting enclosed in four walls, alone, staring, he realized that something beyond thought, beyond control, was running through him. What had triggered it? When? He was aware of a motion, *not* the motion of legal justice which he and his fellow lawyers and judges exercised but some *other* motion—he had no word for it—which seemed to be working under society's impetus but not under its control. It moved that man to run. It moved the media to capture him running. It moved the public to watch him run, just as it had moved her to go to the reporter and to the lawyer. He was convinced that she had not the least idea—none of them had—of what had set her in motion. They would call it what they had always called it, justice. But *he* knew what he was experiencing was not *that* justice but something more. If he were to tell them that, describe it (could he, ever?), they would say he was trying to *avoid* justice when actually he was experiencing *for the first time* something beyond all his and their conception of human justice, something enormous and terrible for which he knew no language. He had entered an unfamiliar terrain invisible to others. He was living on the edge of it. He was divided: he was the man sitting in this room and he was the man he read about each day and watched running on the screen. He was responsible for the man he had never known was inside him whom now he saw clearly there on the screen. He had to hold the two together. He had to run with him because he kept running when he disappeared off the edge of the screen. Now that he had entered that terrain there was no turning back. He could not know what dangers would loom. It was up to him to guide his self through that invisible terrain unknown to both of him. Even with his eyes open, he had entered a darkness fraught with invisible terrors, where he could not move with certainty yet had to keep moving because once he had started he was impelled, he could never stop running. He did not know where his running would take him. Even when he closed his eyes he saw that dark terrain. It moved. He feared its pitfalls might keep him from reaching the other side.

The divorcee allowed no one to interview her. The company forbad any reporters. She left the office only when they assured her no photographer was in sight. Her lawyer had managed a date for the hearing. They had subpoenaed the doctor for the exact dates of the young lawyer's physicals and the results. She kept the children out of sight. Fortunately, nobody had gone to the schools, followed, or harassed them. Indirectly they were probably hurt in ways they would not realize for years. They might one day lose their mother. Wasn't that alone enough? How could she tell them that? She did not discuss damages with anyone but the lawyer. She wanted to keep the public's eye on the dangers of irresponsible sex, the ruin of a life, lives, of which she was a prime example. She would have to live with the consequences for the rest of her life. And nothing on the personal side in your decision to go public? the reporter asked. How could there *not* be anything personal? she replied. But that was not the crucial thing; and suing, the money, was an absolute necessity. She had modest child support from her ex and a regular, modest income as one of hundreds of tech writers; but, with the infection transmitted to her, for how long? And who could know if or when it might appear in the children? She would never trust another man. Anyway who would have her now?

Euphoric, the anchorwoman did not immediately join her cameraman outside the young lawyer's apartment. She was quivering with pleasure from public praise when they went to the car. The lover recognized that she would be a nightmare to be near unless she released that ecstasy in an emotional crescendo. Smiling, seizing the moment, he slipped his hands almost indifferently over her, knowing she would go soft. She sank against him. He kissed her neck, his elbow grazing her breast. Her teeth maddened, he could tongue them, but he was all restraint. The lover knew passion. He knew the anchorwoman. Let her lead. Let her even believe she led. Why not? That freed her appetite. When she let go, she was madness itself. But he did not delude—to achieve such peaks, she had to have a passion outside herself. Work stimulated her passion, but her passion did not replace work. As wretched as that poor bastard the young lawyer was, he was her impetus. Ours, the lover thought. He could not know how long their passion would last, or what would feed her passion next, but right now she was afire with it. Where? he whispered. To your place. And hurry.

The young lawyer stared. He could not stop thinking. Even sitting, he was running. He had to stop *him* or he would never stop running. He would die running. He did not want to die running. The divorcee wanted justice. She was right to want justice. As a lawyer he had sworn to dedicate his life to that, hadn't he? But the divorcee did not know that her action was merely a step in a long motion which even he did not know the true beginning of. He was aware now that he was involved in something nameless that he had never dreamed existed. The divorcee—and the public and press and TV and law courts—would have no conception of what he meant if he said he was experiencing something (a justice?) which in no way shared the concepts of what they called (human?) justice. *He* did not know what he meant, but he was experiencing it. It was an emotional quicksand, and physical: if he dared to step out, the universe might shift and topple. What others could not see was that there was no action of theirs which could answer that motion. Only his could. Only *he* was responsible for his action. And he was responsible for an action that was both his own and *not* his own. He had chosen, and that involved not only his will and the divorcee's will, but also a motion outside themselves; but that did not excuse him from taking the responsibility for both whether or not he was *fully* responsible. Who could understand that who was not in his flesh? *Before* the divorcee's accusation, *he* would not have under-stood that responsibility (for what he did and also for what he did not do) to something he could not yet even define and for which he too had no word, though certainly not human justice. It was that other justice which he must face. And alone. Nobody could face it with him. He had to will himself to face it. Perhaps he had to will himself in the direction of that motion. Perhaps he had to direct that motion. Perhaps that was what his responsibility was, to will that motion his way and triumph over it. Perhaps that was the only way he could be free. Perhaps that was the only way to stop *him* from running and make *him* return to his *self.* You could not live with a divided self.

Something's happening, the reporter said to the photographer. Keep an eye out. The young lawyer had visitors. The reporter had spotted the parents, that friend they had seen go in and out frequently, and the brother, none of whom would give a word. And the anchorwoman, since she would be receiving her award, had told the photographer she had kept on the case, Don't stop watching the house for a minute. I'll get there as soon as I can. Every room in his apartment was lit up, but the blinds drawn. By now the reporter could identify the visitors' cars. Tonight they had all come. Each had arrived with what looked like food, supper. That struck the reporter as strange. Had the young lawyer invited them all? Still, the young lawyer no longer went out to eat but had his groceries brought in, lived and worked virtually under cover, so why not the mercy of family and friends? Mine would do that, the reporter thought, and I would for them. The reporter perched with the photographers, waiting.

The young lawyer had frequently watched the anchorwoman broad-casting the news. But he had never *seen* her until she broadcast *him.* He watched her face, her mouth, but most her eyes, which looked straight at him. Her mouth spewed words. He was a word. Words were objects. Her mouth was chomping objects. She fascinated. Isolated on the screen, she became enormous. And isolated, running like that, he became enormous. Isolated, the house became an object, enormous. And his car. And his of-fice building. He had never *seen* them, not been aware of the enormity of each of them in his life. The newspaper photos isolated him too. He had refused to talk to the reporter and tried to avoid photographers. Now they were always outside. They were isolated objects, enormous too. Obstacles. The terrain out there was filled with them. They came inside through the TV, through the windows, and entered him. When he cut the TV off, they were still there, imprinted on his eye. His mind saw them on the walls, the floor; superimposed on the bed, chairs, stove—everywhere. When he closed his eyes, they appeared, isolated against dark. He could not learn that territory. It was filled with the unknown. But they, TV and newspaper, had made the young lawyer know *him*, that other man in him, for the first time. He realized that now he was the only one in the world who knew *that* him and *this* him. He was the only one who could make them one. It was no question of law, of trials and juries, a judge and a sentence. No. He was on trial with himself and with something in nature which began perhaps centuries before he was born. He had to act, knowing his action would not speak to them. Yet it must be a supremely reasonable action. It must unite those two men forever. He would assume this inordinate punishment, inordinate because he understood part but not all. He understood what he was responsible for but did not understand what he was not responsible for. He understood that he must accept responsibility for both, all, or he was not who he should be, because the law, that law which he practiced, could never fulfill that conception of himself. The law was not adequate to envision what was beyond it, which he had released upon himself by his actions but in *unconscious collusion* with *them*, with *nature*, and with *chance*. He would like to know the *precise* instant in time that the blight had begun. What was responsible? How explain the instant's coincidence of man, rat, flea, bacteria in the bubonic plague? So, he thought, he must be reasonable, he must choose not to be loyal to the law which he had studied for, but to a motion strange and not understood. He must challenge his very makeup, defy whatever was in him, to show that *he*, both of him, could meet the known and the unknown in him and outside him. He could act of his own will and go back purged and pure into that primordial motion.

Though the divorcee would not talk generally about the case, especially at work, keeping a very low profile, she told her intimate friends He's not the man I thought he was. In that cut run on TV again and again, she did not recognize the young lawyer. That was not the man whom her friends had arranged for her to meet at a party, who had slept with her, who had played with the children, whom she had trusted, whom she might one day have married, about whom she thought Mine, a decent repectable man, a lawyer, maybe the stepfather of my children, maybe even the father of my children. But *never*. She could not believe how a word could create instant chaos. For an instant she had not known who she was. Madness. But in the fury of thinking *betrayal lies infection hate death*, thinking *mother, children* saved her. Do anything to save them. She had been reasonable, she thought, to go to the lawyer and to the reporter to expose him, no matter what compensation. It was imperative that people know, that she and the young lawyer become a warning to the public not to be impulsive and irresponsible to themselves and to others. It was near midnight. The children were asleep. She had readied their clothes for school in the morning, and her own. She was lying in bed, thinking about the case as she did every night. She could not avoid it. Her mind was cankered. She knew she would not be able to sleep until something concrete was settled between her and the young lawyer. The phone rang. At this hour! Hello, she said. Something's happened, a strange voice said. What? she said. Who is this?

The parents and the friend and the brother had left the young lawyer's house sometime after eleven and went straight to their cars, ignoring the reporter and the two TV cameramen hanging about the white van, ready with their cameras shouldered. The reporter had taken an hour for a bite with his wife and his little daughter and son, in time to put them to bed, a ritual they loved and he hated to miss; so he felt alert now, patient. Time did not matter. Some fifteen minutes or so after the visitors had left—so the reporter would write for the morning paper—he and the TV cameramen had heard the shot. The lights were still on inside. Initially they saw nothing, but rounding the house they found the back door open. It was the neighbor behind, a woman whose kitchen faced the young lawyer's kitchen on the alley, who had seen the young lawyer's door open and seen him come out and go into the dark alley. Then she heard the shot, and by the time she had opened her back door the reporter and the photographers had already come upon the body of the young lawyer in the alley, dead, the gun lying almost within reach of his hand. He had shot himself in the head. His bloodied face was almost unrecognizable. The reporter was quick to phone the police while the photographers were taking the pictures that would appear on the air and on the front page in the morning, shots of the young lawyer lying in the alley, legs together, arms spread as if embracing the ground, the left side of his head flat against the earth, the side facing the camera mutilated almost to a blur.

What? Shot himself! The anchorwoman clutched her bra. She saw herself in the mirror, naked, holding the bra as if to shield herself from the sight of the voice on the line. Did you get a run on it? she asked the cameraman. Great! She tried to smile, but she had missed it, she was not an eyewitness, the body would be gone, the house cordoned off, the alley and the house empty. The police found a note? What'd it say? Good God! That's the end. I'll be right there. My night! she said to the lover. This night! And me here. The lover could see the fury. The lawyer's shot himself. He left a note saying he blames no one and takes full responsibility for his act. Well, he said, it's a reasonable action given what's left for him here, no future. No future! she cried. She was tense with fury. Why wouldn't she be? She had blown the moment. She had failed to keep her eye on what she must do and who she was. And on *this* of all nights! Quick she was, dressed and ready. She said no word. Her silence seemed to blame him. He was used to that too. Her fury, he knew, came from letting herself stand in the way of a vision of herself. She had waylaid her ambition. She would blame him, but her blame would be a momentary thing. Tomorrow there would be another story. She had an eye for the public's appetite. She was too intelligent not to adapt to the situation and adjust to a new strategy. Don't you think that lawyer knew what he was doing? he said. Whatever he intended, she said, he tricked the divorcee. She won't get a thing out of it. The lover thought Did the young lawyer? But he said nothing. This was not the time.

The divorcee did not go back to bed. She could not stop the voice. Whose voice was it? Anonymous. She saw the young lawyer's face in a moving reel. She could not stop the moving—scenes broken off, interrupted, repeated, continued, fused—an uncontrolled visual history with no chronology, chaotic. Part of her, mechanical, went through breakfast and the children's preparations and the drive to school and then to work.

Part of her stood at the edge of a sudden pit she had never anticipated. A hole. With nothing in it. Nothing. She was the only one who knew the pit was there—and how deep, and empty. At the office nobody mentioned the paper, the news, her situation. Whatever their reaction from the beginning, her fellow workers had been discreet and considerate. She sat, seeing but not seeing. Her lawyer had called early: It's over. We have no case now. His suicide has ended it. Helpless, alone, she sat now in fierce concentration, trying to focus, almost unable to keep from leaping up and crying out to blame him, her friends, herself; to keep from crying out to cry out. She sat, thinking My kids, thinking How'd this come about?, thinking What now? thinking Why? Why me? How could he? Because *he* started it. He shouldn't ever have said. . ., shouldn't have touched me. . . *They* started it, getting me together with him. And I, I shouldn't . . ., shouldn't have . . . But she was not sure *what* she shouldn't have . . . But *he*—How could he do *that*—go, escape, trick her, turn the tables on her, leave her with, as all along he had left her with—how *could* he?—nothing.

Running. Jesus! They said the case was over, but the lover saw the young lawyer in the box again. Jesus! Dead, and they've still got the bastard running. The chronology, clearly outlined on the screen, showed the rapidity of his run, two weeks from his first flight from the photographers to his self-imposed death in the alley. In the last image he looked as if, having run so fast so quickly, he had become exhausted from running and fallen and lay there resting, though the gun told the truth. The lover listened to the anchorwoman's run-down on the young lawyer's history, observing her shimmering always casually perfect hair, her unusual green eyes staring with such conviction into the viewer, into *him,* the lover, those teeth which even when not smiling she could not conceal, exciting him to distraction. But tonight he marveled at nothing so much as her professional detachment, her insistence on not being personally affected, for, as she said, how could she ever do her job? He knew what the young lawyer's suicide meant in her own conception of her place in her profession, her disappointment at not having been able to see this case, ironically, to its legal end. To console, without letting her perceive his subtlety, the lover would lead her through this emotional letdown. Some things you had to hang on to as long as they would last, and he wanted to be sure she believed that *he* believed her at those moments when she envisioned a future after his divorce in a place where her work would take them. She believed he wanted that. Didn't he?

Even now it's not over, the reporter thought. The paper was inundated. For days letters and calls poured in attacking the media: they had driven the young lawyer to suicide; they were irresponsible; they had wrecked the divorcee's life and her chance for a future; they had furthered the rift between the young lawyer and the divorcee; they had not merely played on scandal, but created and fostered it day after day on the front page because sexual infection was a hot issue; they had used it to appeal to politics, religion, and the loss of family values in order to sell papers and make personal and competitive reputations; they had destroyed a life and tarnished the children's lives; they had not lent their media as public use for others, but had used their media destructively against others under the guise of enlightening, warning, and protecting the public, all in the name of truth, of course. Some called it a modern Greek tragedy. Others called it murder, pernicious reporting, betrayal of the moral and ethical bases of good journalism. But the reporter and the paper knew they had the majority on their side: People fed on bad news. But how many wrote letters of praise?

When the lover read the lead news story the day after the suicide, he understood her nervousness. Since, she had not said a word about the letters and calls, though he felt her nerves in every touch of her. She did tell him then what the reporter had said: Today *we're* the victims, it's part of the profession. His general editor had told him This is a community paper. We answer the community. We defend what we stand for, truth. But the public knows that, the reporter had replied, but he knew the public would question what the truth was. The anchorwoman, supporting him in that, said Truth's what we're all about. Our readers shouldn't monkeywrench that. The lover gauged her reactions. He bent himself to console her, even took two days off, announcing that he would demonstrate how fine his culinary art was, smiling, easing her into comfort. Though she was difficult, he rode over her irritations until the paper came and she saw herself and the station and the reporter and the paper vindicated in headlines. The media had done objective reporting. The media were dedicated to giving facts without distortion, and they had responded with facts. The young lawyer had of his own free will chosen a fate which neither the media nor anyone else would have wished for him. . . . And every word of it true, the anchorwoman said, though of course people have a right to their opinion. Who would deny them that? It *was* a messy case. Well . . . The lover feigned indifference, and he *was* concentrating on his soufflé. It's over. Put it behind you. I've got something special for you. He felt her hands go around his waist from behind and run up over his chest. Have you? Again he feigned indifference. Yes, but it's very delicate and requires just the right heat and I have to be very careful not to mix too much flour in it and must pour it at just the right consistency and take it out of the oven at just the right moment or the thing will fall flat as nothing. We can't have that.

GEORGE ALBON's most recent book is *Thousands Count Out Loud* from lyric& press. He lives in San Francisco.

WILL ALEXANDER has recent and forthcoming work in *Sulfur, Faucheuse, Terra Nova, Conjunctions,* and *Syllogism.* A new book, *Exobiology as Goddess,* is forthcoming from Manifest Press.

STEFANI BARBER lives in San Francisco. Her work has appeared or is forthcoming in *Ante Up, Kenning, Mungo vs. Ranger, Syllogism, TRIPWIRE,* and *Step into a World: A Global Anthology of the New Black Literature.* She holds an M.F.A. from San Francisco State University.

REBECCA BERG was born in Cincinatti, Ohio, in 1962. A former cellist, she has degrees in English from Oberlin College and Cornell University. Currently, she lives in Denver and copyedits the *Journal of Environmental Health.* "A History of Song," excerpted from a novel in progress, is her first published work of fiction.

MEI-MEI BERSSENBRUGGE was born in 1947 in Beijing, China and grew up in Massachusetts. Her books include *Empathy* (Station Hill Press), *Endocrinology* (Kelsey St. Press), and *Four Year Old Girl* (Kelsey St. Press). She is the recipient of two National Endowment for the Arts fellowships, the Asian-American Writers Award, and the Western States Book Award. She lives in New York with the artist Richard Tuttle and their daughter, Martha.

EILEEN O MALLEY CALLAHAN is currently working on a Ph.D. dissertation in the English Department at UC Berkeley on the imagination of reading. A collection of poems called *The Materials* will be published early next year.

CYDNEY CHADWICK is the author of seven books/chapbooks, the most recent being a revised edition of *Persistent Disturbances.* A recipient of the New American Fiction Award, a Gertrude Stein Award in Innovative American Poetry, and a creative writing fellowship from the California Arts Council, she lives in the countryside about fifty miles north of San Francisco. She has been managing Avec publications since 1988.

PATRICIA DIENSTFREY is co-founder of Kelsey St. Press, which has been publishing innovative writing by women since 1974 and collaborations between poets and visual artists since the 1980s. Her most recent book, *The Woman Without Experiences* (Kelsey St., 1995), was winner of The America Award for Literature in 1996. Her work appears in *Moving Borders: Three*

Decades of Innovative Writing by Women, edited by Mary Margaret Sloan (Talisman House, 1997). Currently, with Brenda Hillman, she is co-editing a collection of essays entitled *New Writings on Poetics and Motherhood.* She is the mother of three grown sons and lives with her husband, Ted, in Berkeley, California.

TIMOTHA DOANE was born in Corpus Christi, Texas in 1944. She grew up in Connecticut. She lives in Bernal Heights, San Francisco and teaches American English to speakers of other languages at City College.

GARY DUEHR has published work in *Appalachee Quarterly, Cottonwood,* the *Iowa Review* and others. He has an M.F.A. from the University of Iowa and a collection, *Winter Light,* was published from Four Way Books in 1999.

AJA COUCHOIS DUNCAN lives in the Santa Cruz Mountains where she practices the three R's: reading, running, and writing, and teaches poetry through California Poets in the Schools. Her writing has been published in *Clamour, Fourteen Hills, Mirage/Period(ical), Prosodia, San Jose Manual of Style, Superflux,* and *Transfer.* New work is forthcoming in *Mungo vs. Ranger* and on-line at *Narrativity* and *Blithehouse.* Aja is a graduate of the M.F.A. creative writing program at San Francisco.

KENDALL DUNKELBERG teaches literature and writing at Mississippi University for Women. His translations have recently appeared in *The Literary Review, Fine Madness,* and *Two Lines.* Green Integer Press published his translation of poems by Paul Snoek, the trilogy *Hercules, Richelieu,* and *Nostradamus.* Florida Literary Foundation Press will publish a book of his own poems, *Landscapes and Architectures,* this year.

BETSY FAGIN is the author of two chapbooks, *Watch the Blue Language* and *Physical Culture.* She edits and maintains website presst.org from Brooklyn, New York. Recent work appears at theeastvillage.com and The Poetry Project website, and is forthcoming in *Fence.*

H. E. FRANCIS is the author of several collections of stories—including *The Itinerary of Beggars* and *A Disturbance of Gulls* (Braziller). He has won numerous awards and been anthologized, notably in the O. Henry, Best American, and Pushcart Prize collections.

RENEE GLADMAN was born in 1971 in Atlanta, Georgia and now lives in San Francisco, where she edits the chapbook press, Leroy. She is the author of

Arlem (Idiom Press, 1996) and *Not Right Now* (Second Story Books, 1998). *Juice,* a collection of prose, will be published by Kelsey St. Press.

BRENDA HILLMAN's five collections of poetry—*White Dress* (1985), *Fortress* (1989), *Death Tractates* (1992), *Bright Existence* (1993), and *Loose Sugar* (1997) have been published by Wesleyan University Press. She is on the faculty of St. Mary's College in Moraga, California where she teaches literature and creative writing, and serves on the permanent faculties of Squaw Valley Community of Writers and of Napa Valley Writers' Conference.

CAROL HINRICHSEN was born and raised in Iowa where she got degrees in Graphic Design and Art Education. Last May she received an M.F.A. from Johnson State College and she recently left her position at the Vermont Studio Center to return to the world of computers.

JACK HIRSCHMAN has just returned to the Bay Area from a reading tour in Italy and a residency in France. He recently published *Eleven Poems* of Franco Carlini, translated for the C.C. Marimba Press of Berkeley.

DAVID HUFFMAN lives and works in Berkeley, CA, where he was born in 1963. A recipient of an M.F.A. in 1998 from the California College of Arts and Crafts, he has exhibited in San Francisco at Patricia Sweetow Gallery and Southern Exposure and in Los Angeles at the Municipal Art Gallery, Jan Baum Gallery, La Luz de Jesus Gallery, and Julie Recco Gallery. Mr. Huffman is represented by Patricia Sweetow Gallery, San Francisco.

GIGI JANCHANG was born in China and raised in Taiwan. She received her M.F.A. from the San Francisco Art Institute and her site-specific installations have been exhibited in Germany, Sweden, and the Bay Area.

ALICE JONES's books are *The Knot, Anatomy,* and *Isthmus.* Her poems have appeared in *Volt, Ploughshares, Pequod, Chelsea,* and ZYZZYVA.

GEORGE KALAMARAS's poems appear in *Best American Poetry 1997, Boulevard, Epoch, Hambone, The Iowa Review, New Letters, Sulfur, TriQuarterly,* and elsewhere. He is the author of two poetry chapbooks, and his first full-length collection, *The Theory and Function of Mangoes,* won the 1998 Four Way Books Intro Series in Poetry Award and was published by Four Way Books in 2000. Among his awards are a 1993 N.E.A. Poetry Fellowship and the 2000 Abiko Quarterly (Japan) Poetry Award. In 1994 he spent several months in India on a Fulbright Indo-U.S. Advanced Research Fellowship.

BHANU KAPIL RIDER's prose chapbook, *Autobiography of a Cyborg,* was published by Leroy Press in September 2000. Her book, *The Vertical Interrogation of Strangers,* is forthcoming from Kelsey St. Press. She has also recently started a chapbook series under the imprint of Wolfgirl Press. Kapil Rider is of Indian origin and grew up in London and the Punjab. She currently lives in Colorado.

W. B. KECKLER was an N.E.A. fellow sometime in the last millennium. His books include *Ants Dissolve in Moonlight* and *Recombinant Image Day.*

LYNN MARIE KIRBY has been working with ideas of intimate and cultural landscapes across the materials of film, video, sound and light for almost two decades. Her work has been shown at festivals in London, Athens, Istanbul and Oberhausen; she has had one-person shows in the Museum of Modern Art and Artist Space in New York, George Pompidou Centre and Théâtre de L'Entrepôt in Paris, LACE in LA, the San Francisco Cinématheque and Pacific Film Archive in Berkeley.

ANDREW LINDSAY is an Australian writer who has worked in journalism and theater, as well as been an oral historian in various working class communities in Melbourne. His short story "The Peanut Man" was a winner of the Radio National Books and Writing Short Story competition. His first novel, *The Breadmaker's Carnival,* is published by Allen and Unwin in Australia and won the Fellowship of Australian Writers (Vic) Jim Hamilton Award. It will be published by The Ecco Press at the end of 2000.

MEDBH MCGUCKIAN was born in Belfast where she lives with her family. She is the author of numerous books, most recently, *Shelmalier,* published by The Gallery Press. Among the prizes she has won are England's National Poetry Competition, The Cheltenham Award, The Rooney Prize, and the Bass Ireland Award for literature.

TRINH T. MINH-HA is a filmmaker, writer, composer and Professor of Film, Women's Studies and Rhetoric at the University of California, Berkeley. Her award-winning and internationally acclaimed work includes seven books, a volume of poetry, a multi-media installation *Nothing But Ways* (in collaboration), and five feature-length films that have been honored in twenty-four retrospectives around the world.

FRED MOTEN was born and raised in Las Vegas and now lives in New York City where he is assistant professor of Performance Studies in the Tisch

School of the Arts, New York University. He has published poetry in *Grand Street, Lift,* and has poems forthcoming in *Callaloo.* His first chapbook, *Arkansas,* was published last year by Pressed Wafer Press.

DENISE NEWMAN's latest book of poetry is *Human Forest* (Apogee Press). She currently teaches at Mills College.

JENIE PAK received her M.F.A. in Poetry from Cornell University, and has work published or forthcoming in *Alligator Juniper, Love Shook My Heart II, Many Mountains Moving,* and *The Oakland Review.* She lives in San Francisco.

MONICA PECK's poems have appeared in *The Pleasure Beast, Pressed Wafer,* and *First Intensity* magazines. A native Kansan, she currently lives in San Francisco.

V. PENELOPE PELLIZON has published poems in *The Nation, The Iowa Review, Ploughshares, The Formalist,* and *ZYZZYVA.* She was a recipient of the Discovery Award, sponsored by *The Nation* in 1997.

IRENE PIJOAN's work has been shown at the Guggenheim Museum, the Corcoran Gallery in Washington, D.C., the Oakland Museum, and the Berkeley Art Museum. Her awards include a National Endowment for the Arts, and Art Matters grants, and residencies at Roswell, New Mexico and Djerassi in Woodside, California. She is represented by the Rena Bransten Gallery in San Francisco.

LISA RAPPOPORT is a letterpress printer who publishes artist's books and broadsides under the imprints Trouser Press and Littoral Press. She is the editor of *Letters from Wupatki,* letters by Courtney Reeder Jones, who lived and worked at a remote national monument in Arizona in the 1930s and '40s (The University of Arizona Press, 1995). Rappoport won the Icarus Poetry Competition in 1998.

ELÉNA RIVERA was born in Mexico City and spent her childhood in Paris, Fance. *Unknowne Land,* her book-length poem which is excerpted here, was recently published by Kelsey St. Press. She is also the author of two chapbooks, *Wale; or, the Corse* (Leave Books, 1995) and *The Wait; for Homer's Penelope* (Em Press, 1994). She won first prize in the 1998 Stand Magazine International Poetry Competition. She lives in New York City.

ELIZABETH ROBINSON's most recent book, *House Made of Silver,* is forthcoming from Kelsey St. Press. She has work forthcoming in *Volt, Fence,* and *Crayon,* and her recent chapbooks include *Lodger* and *As Betokening.*

JAIME ROBLES is a book artist and writer. She also publishes under the name of Carla Lemos.

JAMES SACRÉ was born in Vendée in 1939 to a peasant family, and moved to the United States in 1972. He has just returned to France after retiring from Smith College. His publications of or around poetry include over thirty titles in French. In 1988 he was awarded France's top poetry prize, the Prix Apollinaire.

SANDRO SARDELLA is a noted poet and painter from the Varese area of Italy. A book of his poems, *Colored Paper Bits,* was published in the United States in 1998. He has exhibited widely in Italy.

JONO SCHNEIDER co-edits *Untitled,* a magazine of prose poetry, and Instance Press. Recent work appears in *6ix, Tinfish,* and *Aufgabe.*

giovanni singleton writes, teaches, and collects bookmarks in the San Francisco Bay Area. Her poetry has appeared in *Mirage #4/Period(ical), Chain, Local Howlers, KENNING,* and on the building of the Yerba Buena Center for the Arts in San Francisco.

PAUL SNOEK (1933-1981) is the pseudonym of Edmund Schietekat, one of Belgium's best-known postwar poets. He published twenty volumes of poetry between 1954 and 1982, and received many prizes, including Belgium's Triennial State Prize for Poetry in 1968. He was a director of the Flemish P.E.N. Center and was also known as a painter. A member of the second experimental generation in Flanders, his early work was influenced by Flemish expressionism and French surrealism. His later work was both introspective and satirical. He died in an automobile accident in 1981.

PHYLLIS STOWELL has published *Assent to Solitude, Who is Alice,* and *Sequence and Consequence,* as well as traditional and innovative poetry in a wide range of reviews. Professor Emerita from St. Mary's College in Moraga, she was a founding member of the M.F.A. program there. She is co-editor of an anthology of women's poetry to be published in 2002.

COLE SWENSEN's recent books includes *Oh,* from Apogee Press (2000) and *Try,* from the University of Iowa Press (1999). *Such Rich Hour,* from which these poems are taken, will be published by Iowa in the fall of 2001.

SUSAN THACKREY's work has appeared in *Avec, Hambone, Talisman,* and other magazines. Her book, *Empty Gate,* was published in 1999 by Listening Chamber Press.

AMY TRACHTENBERG, a visual artist living in San Francisco, recently designed the theater sets for *A Little Girl Dreams of Taking the Veil,* a new opera which premiered at ODC Theater. Her collaborations with poets can be seen in the wide world of the small press.

ROBIN TREMBLAY-MCGAW co-edits *Lipstick Eleven* and The Forum section won class and innovative writing for *HOW2* (fall 1999).

LUKE TRENT is a poet and photographer. In 1996 he won the Joseph Henry Jackson Award for his manuscript *Love of the Game.* His poems have appeared in *Volt, Columbia Poetry Review, Fence,* and *Northwest Review,* among other publications.

ROSMARIE WALDROP's most recent books of poems are *Reluctant Gravities* (New Directions, 1999), *Split Infinites* (Singing Horse Press, 1998), and *Another Language: Selected Poems* (Talisman House, 1997).

CHRISTOPHE WALL-ROMANA has written precious little poetry since entering the doctoral program in French at Berkeley. His translations of Sacré's work have appeared in the journal of French studies, *Sites.* His as yet unpublished *Come, Someone Says* is the first book of James Sacré's to be translated into English.

ELIZABETH WILLIS is the author of *The Human Abstract* (Penguin, 1995) and *Second Law* (Avenue B, 1993). She teaches at Mills College.

The theme for *Five Fingers Review, Issue 20* will be "The Garden." Please send submissions to:

> *Five Fingers Review*
> P.O. Box 12955
> Berkeley, CA 94712-3955

before November 2001 in order to be considered for publication in this issue. We are also very interested in publishing reviews and studies of author's works. Our email address is jrobles@best.com; however, we do not accept electronic submissions at this time.

If you are interested in subscribing to *Five Fingers Review,* please send inquiries to:

> Subscriptions
> *Five Fingers Review*
> 652 Woodland Ave.
> San Leandro, CA 94577